CONTENTS

INDEX OF CHARACTERS

TEXTUAL INDEX

women of the new testament

30 Devotional Messages
for Women's Groups

by

ABRAHAM KUYPER, D.D., LL.D.

Translated from the Dutch
by Henry Zylstra

Daybreak Books

Zondervan Publishing House
Grand Rapids, Michigan

Dedicated by the publishers
to our wives
MARY AND WILMA
and to our sister
ANNA MARIE

WOMEN OF THE NEW TESTAMENT
Copyright © 1934 / Renewal 1962 by
Zondervan Publishing House
Grand Rapids, Michigan

Daybreak Books are published by Zondervan
Publishing House, 1415 Lake Drive, S.E.,
Grand Rapids, Michigan 49506

ISBN 0-310-36751-4

Printed in the United States of America

90 91 92 93 94 / EP / 46 45 44 43

ELISABETH

*And, behold, thy cousin Elisabeth, she hath also conceived
a son in her old age: and this is the sixth month with her
who was called barren.*

—LUKE 1:36.

READ: LUKE 1

ELISABETH is the person who can be praised as the first
woman, first even before Mary, who confessed Christ
in the flesh. When Mary, after she had conceived by the
Spirit, came to her, Elisabeth exclaimed in prophetical
prayer and prayerful prophecy: "Whence is this to me, that
the mother of my Lord should come to me?" By that
unexpected and unhesitating confession she strengthened
Mary's faith in the fact that she did, indeed, bear the
Saviour of the world in her bosom.

It is that strong and thorough-going faith which constitutes Elisabeth's most pronounced virtue. Perhaps her firm
conviction that Christ had actually begun to assume human
form does not strike us as being particularly remarkable.
This might seem so to us because we know that Mary
actually bore her firstborn child, and that He indeed proved
to be the Mediator between God and man. But Elisabeth
did not have this historical perspective, and for that reason
the unhesitating conviction to which she gave expression is
truly remarkable.

5

Israel had almost dwindled into nothingness because of the scorn and malice of the Roman jurisdiction. The worship of Jehovah had become little more than sheer formalism. Caiaphas, for instance, constitutes an object lesson in the degenerate condition of the priesthood at this time. And we must remember that Elisabeth was part and parcel of this spiritually emasculated epoch.

Besides, Elisabeth was old, and was a woman who for many years had prayed God for a child. She was scorned and designated as a disgrace because of her childless state. Then too, she had not been present at the time that the Angel appeared to Zacharias. She had not heard what Gabriel told Mary. All these matters were reported to her only by hearsay; they were rumors which had reached her ears.

In spite of these untoward circumstances, however, Elisabeth immediately transcended all doubt and hesitation. She not only hoped for the Messiah's coming, but she believed it. When Mary came to her, she at once saw and believed this wonderful truth, "There, beneath that woman's clothes, my Saviour is concealed." The Messiah was no more to come. Elisabeth knew that He already was, that He existed in Mary's womb. Hence, she prayed to Him, and confessed Him.

The steps by which the Lord led Elisabeth to this full, rich faith are by no means concealed from us. She bore the same name that had been given to Aaron's wife, and she was a descendant of one of Aaron's daughters. Caiaphas, we said, serves as a striking example of the degeneracy of the priesthood at this time. Over against him Elisabeth represents a true sapling from Aaron's family trunk. She preserved all the blessed traditions of Aaron and his family. The Lord, therefore, had led her along the ways of feminine shame and humiliation, for we must remember that it was a special disgrace for the daughter of a priest to remain childless.

Thereupon the Lord suddenly blessed her with an unhoped for pregnancy. It came when she had given up all hope of ever bearing a child. Her conception was accompanied by an Angel's message, and by the muteness of her husband. It is pathetic but true that Zacharias could not tell her anything about that meeting with the Angel; he had to write it. From these unusual demonstrations Elisabeth knew that God had again chosen to accomplish miraculous things. To her it seemed that the days of Abraham and Sarah had returned, and that God had sought for His people once more.

Mary came to her after Elisabeth had quietly bided her time for five months. Elisabeth's maternal instinct told her that a child stirred in her womb at her meeting Mary, and that that child stirred in an extraordinary way. Thus the mother and the child were each affected by the influence of the Holy Ghost because of the Saviour's approach. At once the flower of faith completely blossomed forth in Elisabeth. She appreciated and felt the bliss of facing the wonderful fact that God, revealed in the flesh, was fulfilling the Hope of the fathers.

It is interesting to observe the evidence of that faith in Elisabeth. She was the mother of John. Mary, a woman much younger than she, and one who had not even descended from the family of priests, was the mother of the Messiah. It seems natural that this situation would have induced the jealousy and sinfulness of the human heart to ask, "Why couldn't I have the greater honor?" We know that old women are frequently inclined to be jealous of those who are younger. But, in Elisabeth such thoughts were completely suppressed. She gave Mary the most honorable of names: "Mother of the Lord." And she gave Mary that name spontaneously and unaffectedly. She praised Mary unstintedly as one "blessed among women." Her son said later, "He must increase, but I must decrease." The spirit of John permeated his mother at the time she ascribed to Mary the honor that is above all honors. Elisabeth, we said, was the last sapling to spring from the soil of Aaron's house, who fulfilled the holy vocation which God called that family to fulfil. Judah was to give birth to the Messiah, but Aaron was to worship Him in service.

SUGGESTED QUESTIONS FOR STUDY AND DISCUSSION

1. Who in the flesh, first confessed Christ?
2. How do we know that Elisabeth had sincere faith?
3. How do we know that she brought up her son in the fear of the Lord?

MARY

(1)

Her Lowliness

For He hath regarded the low estate of His handmaiden: for, behold, from henceforth all generations shall call me blessed.

—Luke 1:48.

Read: Luke 1

MARY, the Mother of our Lord, was also the daughter of a king. Christ was born from her and from her alone. The Holy Apostle Paul affirms that Christ was "of the seed of David according to the flesh." And even though the genealogies of Matthew and Luke terminate with the name of Joseph, it was only through Mary that Christ could be a son of David according to the flesh.

The fact that Mary was Elisabeth's cousin by no means makes it impossible to believe that she was of royal birth. It is true that Elisabeth was a descendant of Levi and that the sons of the priests usually married members of the same tribe. But this did not constitute a hard and fast rule. It was perfectly possible for Judah and Levi to become brothers-in-law.

Mary was, therefore, the daughter of a king. Because of that, her lowliness is particularly conspicuous. There is nothing disgraceful about belonging to the lower classes, of course. It is not a shame to be married to a carpenter. But if royal blood courses in one's veins, if one's true rank is that of a princess, and one's appropriate home a palace, then

9

the privations of circumstance become very real. It still happens frequently that a person of a high station in life suddenly falls to a lower plane of social and economic living. Such people usually become grim and bitter, and fail altogether to live positively. Their privations cause them to bear a "grudge against the universe." But limiting circumstances in the case of some people serve as a blessing. Such people then learn to observe a proper humility over against God, and tend to develop the finer culture of the soul as a result.

In this same way, circumstances proved to be a blessing to Joseph, and even more so to Mary, the Mother of our Lord. For centuries the Roman Catholic Church has believed, and since 1879 it has confessed, that the conception of Mary was also miraculous. The implications of this doctrine are that Mary's person was not cursed by original sin, and that she, accordingly, was born without original guilt and without original pollution. To this conception of her birth there is generally added the doctrine that she never sinned in her later life. According to this view Mary stands apart from the rest of the sinful human race. Such are the implications of the doctrine of the Immaculate Conception.

If we question upon what basis this confession can be made, we are pointed to a single passage in Luke 1:28. We read there that Gabriel told Mary: "Blessed art thou among women." In the Greek original this whole prediction is expressed by a single word, namely, *Kecharitomene*. Origen interpreted this as meaning that a certain special grace accrued to Mary even before her birth. Granted, that this were true, the same could be said of John the Baptist, for he received the Holy Spirit before birth. And yet, John the Baptist was not born immaculately pure. The Roman Catholic theologians have cited the Church fathers as additional evidence for their doctrine. But the statements of these prove meaningless in all instances in which they are not based upon the Word of God. Besides, these theologians contradict themselves. If it was possible for Mary to be born unpolluted from sinful parents, why, by the same reasoning, should it not have been possible for the Christ?

However, a far weightier argument must be advanced against this doctrine of the Immaculate Conception. If that doctrine were true, the work of salvation would be quite superfluous. If it were possible for Mary to be born immaculate and to remain sinless throughout life because of grace, then the same ends could have been accomplished for all men immediately after the fall by that same grace. Then sin would at once have become a non-entity, and the Mediator's coming would have been entirely unnecessary.

For us, therefore, the lowliness of Mary retains a dual significance. She occupied a low estate to illustrate how a princess from the house of David had fallen from her high position. And she served to illustrate, besides, how the whole race had fallen from its high place in Paradise to the lower planes of sin and guilt.

Suggested Questions for Study and Discussion

1. What is meant by the lowliness of Mary?
2. Why was it necessary for her to take on this state?
3. What is meant by the Roman Catholic doctrine of the "Immaculate Conception"

MARY

(2)

THE MOTHER OF OUR LORD

For He that is mighty hath done to me great things; and holy is his name.

—LUKE 1:49.

READ: LUKE 2

IN her song of praise Mary sang that great things had been done to her by Him that was mighty, and she said that His name was Holy. Her praise was by no means exaggerated. It is inconceivable, we feel sure, that any higher or more beautiful honor could have accrued to anyone than that which Mary was permitted to receive. She was truly the most blessed among women. Of all the children of men she was chosen to be overshadowed by the power of the Highest in a special sense. Throughout the centuries the true Church has conceded to her the name, Mother of God. We can have no objection to that, provided, of course, that name be rightly interpreted.

It may not be said that she merely gave her flesh and blood to the Christ, and that we may never look for anything noble or sacred in that flesh and blood. We know that the Scriptures themselves take the lead in singing Mary's praise. The Angel said that she had been favored by the Lord. Elizabeth greeted her as one "blessed among women," and called her blessed because she had believed (vs. 45). And Mary herself was so conscious of the rich blessedness that had become hers, that she exclaimed: "From henceforth all generations shall call me blessed." For that reason we may not, in reacting against the Roman

12

and Greek Catholic over-emphasis of her glory, judge wrongly about her.

Mary was an elect of God in a unique sense. Her privilege was greater than was ever given any human being. And the striking aspect of her glory is that its brightest lustre was reflected by the dark shadow of her lowliness. We must not stress the point beyond this however. We must beware of detracting from her essential glory by all kinds of imagined creations.

The unique favor which was granted her was that she might be the Mother of our Lord, that the Son of God took His human form from her flesh and blood, and that it was her privilege to drink love from His holy eyes during the many years in which He, still unknown to the world, was a child in her home. That honor was not granted to her because she had earned it, but because God's sovereignty designated that she should be the recipient of it. He had selected Mary for that purpose. He saved her life, and He sent her His Angel to acquaint her with heaven's message.

Hence, there is no reason to praise her because of the extraordinary abundance of grace which was given her. Not Mary, but the Lord God must be praised because of the grace which He gave her. The very essence of grace demands this. Grace bars the possibility of human credit and pride. We may not be praised for the grace we have received. Grace is no longer grace the moment our own virtue of effort achieves something.

True, Mary was a most highly favored and blessed woman because of the unique distinction that became hers. For that reason we can praise her fortune, and, like Elisabeth, we can bless her. We can be grateful for the grace that was granted her, and for the grace which through her was granted to each of us. All that grace does not remove the fact, however, that Mary was the handmaiden of the

Lord. In thinking of her, the simple burden of our song must be: "Glory be God's in the highest!"

We have not said anything, however, which would make it unreasonable to believe that this blessed woman soared to heaven even as Elijah did. But the Church can learn nothing about that from the Scriptures. Hence, whatever the Roman Catholic Church relates about it is based not upon God's Word but upon traditions. No one knew where Mary was buried. It was thought that if she had been buried upon the earth the place of her interment would have become known. Besides, it was hard for many to accept the fact that the body of Mary, out of which the Son of God had taken His human form, should have been subjected to disintegration in the grave. For these reasons some believed that Mary had died, that she had risen again, and that she very soon after ascended to heaven. Such arguments seem to be an attempt to glorify her in the same manner in which Christ is glorified.

This tradition is, however, very uncertain. In the Occident we speak of "Mary's Ascension Day." In Oriental countries, people give that same day a name which means "to die" or "to fall asleep." It seems that the Occident at first also spoke of the "Dormitio Mariæ" a name which refers to Mary's having fallen asleep. Later this conception was replaced by another, and the name was changed to "Assumptio Mariæ." This was intended to refer to Mary's ascension.

SUGGESTED QUESTIONS FOR STUDY AND DISCUSSION

1. Why do we say that Mary was "blessed among women"
2. Why was this privilege granted to Mary?
3. Was Mary conscious of this privilege? How do we know?

MARY

(3)

HER FAITH

Blessed is she that believed: for there shall be a perform-ance of those things which were told her from the Lord.
                                        —LUKE 1:45.

READ LUKE 1:45-55

THE undue religious exaltation of the Mother of the Lord is based, primarily, upon her faith, and upon her faith conceived of as a personal accomplishment. When Mary received the glorious announcement of the Angel, she answered: "Behold the handmaid of the Lord; be it unto me according to thy Word." Elisabeth affirmed concerning that very confession: "Blessed is she that believed: for there shall be a performance of things that were told her from the Lord." The faith to which Mary gave expression has not always been thought of as having been freely given her by grace. It is thought by some that Mary partly accomplished it herself. Wherever this conception prevails, these corollaries follow: The incarnation of the Lord was made possible only by Mary's assent; by making that incarnation possible, Mary enabled Christ to offer the supreme sacrifice of redemption; and that for these reasons, Mary is partly to be praised for the redemption of the world, and for the forgiveness of our sins by the blood of the Lamb.

Do not interpret our efforts to oppose these conceptions as an attempt to detract from the quality of Mary's faith. Such an attempt would be hostile to the spirit of the Scriptures. No one can doubt that her confession to the Angel

15

was an act of faith. We know that Elisabeth, in a holy rapture, confirmed that faith. Hence, the only matter we object to in such unwarranted exaltation of Mary is that it departs from the rule: "Faith is not of yourselves, it is the gift of God."

Mary's faith, too, was not of herself. Only by the grace of God did she make that noble confession. And this is a formulation of a truth which diametrically opposes that which maintains that Mary enabled God to complete His determinate counsel. We insist that God the Lord, in order to fulfil that counsel, exerted an influence upon Mary's soul and upon her body. He influenced her soul by giving her faith, and her body by building up that of the Saviour from her flesh and blood.

Mary's virginity is sometimes referred to as another of her exceptional virtues. But the Scriptures give us no reason to believe that she remained a virgin. There is no text which informs us that Mary's giving birth to her Child left her maidenhood untrammeled. The reference to Jesus' having entered through "closed doors" is not relevant in the matter. And there is nothing which justifies an interpretation of Ezekiel 44:2 as a reference to Mary's virginity. We read there concerning the door on the east side of the sanctuary: "This gate shall be shut, it shall not be opened and no man shall enter in by it: because the Lord, the God of Israel, hath entered in by it, therefore it shall be shut." What right have we to apply the meaning of these words to Mary? But, granted that we had that right, the sense of them, moreover, indicates that the door was opened when the Lord entered. Besides, the third verse indicates that the prince could also enter by the gate.

These arguments are not being advanced in order to make it seem plausible that Mary bore other children after the miracle at Bethlehem. It will never be conclusively determined whether or not she did bear other children. Nothing can be inferred from the fact that we read about the "brothers of Jesus." The word "brother" is used in the Bible not only to denote a brother by birth, but also to designate a step-brother, or, for the matter of that, to point out any relative (Gen. 3:18; 14:16; 29:12; Num. 8:26; 15:10, etc.). But these arguments are included in order to show that it cannot be proved from the example of Mary that God prefers a virgin to a mother. In spite of that, however, it remains true, that she combined the tender love of a virgin with the rich, luxurious life of a mother.

No matter how highly we esteem Mary as the Mother of the Lord and as the Chosen One of God, it can never be demonstrated from the Scriptures that she was an extraordinarily spiritual woman. She is mentioned fifteen times in the Bible after the account of the events which took place at Bethlehem. When Jesus was twelve years old, she went with Him to the Temple of Zion. At that time she did not understand Jesus. We see her again at the marriage of Cana. Here again she indicated that she could not understand the profound thoughts of Jesus. Later, when she wished to rescue Jesus from the masses (Matt. 12:46), He was compelled to reprimand her by pointing to the people of God and saying of them: "See my mother." At Golgotha she certainly had a splendid opportunity to reveal the depth of her spiritual penetration, but there again she gave expression to nothing which any mother might not express. When Jesus had ascended to heaven we find that Mary also belonged to the group of believers (Acts 1:14). In the description of that group, however, we find that the Apostles are named first, then the other women, and finally the mother of Jesus. She seems to have been of less significance than they.

The Apostles, neither on Pentecost nor on any other day, ever mentioned Mary's name in preaching Christ. Paul, who received his gospel directly from Jesus, does not even mention her name. Neither in the Acts nor in the Epistles of the Apostles is any kind of honor ascribed to her. Her opinion is not asked for upon any occasion. She disappeared from the Scriptures inconspicuously. Whoever compared the position which the Roman and Greek Catholic Churches give Mary in their worship and in the heart of their religion with the silence maintained about her in the Acts and the Epistles, cannot avoid thinking that the Apostolic fathers thought about her in the same way that our Reformed theologians do. Among these her position was quite inferior to that to which the Roman Catholic Church very early exalted her.

SUGGESTED QUESTIONS FOR STUDY AND DISCUSSION

1. Why is Mary to be partly praised for the redemption of the world?
2. Have we any Scriptural proof of Mary's remaining a virgin after the birth of Christ?
3. Was Mary an exceptionally spiritual woman?

ANNA

And she, coming in that instant, gave thanks likewise unto the Lord, and spake of Him to all them that looked for redemption in Jerusalem.

—LUKE 2:38.

READ: LUKE 2:36-38

ALL the glory of Jesus' birth concentrated itself in the ancient kingdom of Judah. Both Joseph and Mary had descended from the tribe of Judah. Elisabeth lived in Judah, and in Judah John was born. And Bethlehem, the city in which the manger was found and to which the Angel came down, was also in Judah's tribe.

Irrespective of that, however, Jesus came for the whole of Israel, and He came for more than Israel for He was also to serve as a light unto the heathen. The Magi came as the representatives of heathendom to greet the newborn King. And Anna, the prophetess in the Temple, came to confess the Hope of the fathers for that part of Israel which lay outside of the proper domains of Judah. She was not a descendant of Judah's tribe. She was the daughter of Phanuel, of the tribe of Aser. And Aser was situated among the dispersed tribes of Israel. For that reason her office in the Temple has a real significance. Under Jeroboam the Ten Tribes had emancipated themselves from David's House, and had, throughout the centuries after that time, persevered in rejecting Israel's Messiah and God's covenant. Now we observe that Anna appears in the Temple beside the figure of Simeon to greet the King of the House of David. It almost seems as if she came to call Him to the Lake of Genesareth and to the despised Galilee,

19

in order that He might again gather a proudly rebellious people into His Kingdom.

Simeon and Anna were both old people. In fact, Anna was eighty-four years old. For that reason it cannot be said that she, any more than did Simeon, represented the younger generation. She did not belong to the circle out of which the Lord chose His disciples, nor did she belong to the group out of which He selected Mary and Martha. On the contrary, she represented the dying Israel. Anna extended the palm of honor to the Christ as a representative of the past, not as that of the future. It seems as if she came to lay the offering of thanksgiving of forty generations at Jesus' feet before she died.

Anna brought this offering as a woman, after Simeon had preceded with his as a man. Thus we observe again that both sexes, together and individually, are called to glorify the God of Israel. Beside Abraham we find Sarah, beside Barak we find Deborah, and beside Moses, Zipporah. In this same way, Anna, who came from Aser, stood beside Simeon. That does not mean, however, that she was the wife of Simeon. Doubtless, they lived in a relationship in which an intense spiritual unity obliterated sexual difference. Long before, perhaps some sixty years before, she had been married for a short time, but after that she had not married again. After that time she had secluded herself in the Temple in order to be a door-keeper in the House of the Lord. We read that she "departed not from the temple, but served God with fastings and prayers night and day." She must have lived a life of genuine if conspicuous piety, and she must have had an unconscious premonition of the things which were to happen, for she must have heard Simeon say that the Christ should come even before his death.

We have said that Anna came from Aser, and that she was Simeon's feminine aide at the Temple. We must observe, besides, that she was a prophetess, and that as such she is to be included with that continuous line of prophets and prophetesses who had heralded the coming of the Prophet and Teacher throughout the epochs. Jesus was born from the tribe of Kings. Zacharias and Elisabeth represented the time-honored tribe of the Priests, and Anna is another woman who represented the spiritual officials in Israel. Christ, then, represented the tribe of the Kings, Zacharias and Elisabeth that of the Priests, and beside these, Anna appeared to represent the Prophets. Prophecy had prophesied His coming. Now that He had come, it seems that this last of the prophetesses had to arrive in order to confirm that this, indeed, was the Holy Child whose coming had been announced by the Isaiahs and Malachis. For we read that she not only confessed the Christ, but also that "she spake of Him to all them that looked for redemption in Jerusalem."

Thus it was whispered about in the Temple that the hour of redemption was at hand, that the fulness of time had come, and that the Saviour of the world should arise out of that holy child. When Anna had confirmed that, her task had been fulfilled. Her testimony in the Temple was the last voice of prophecy that was ever heard. Prophecy had served its purpose. John, the Herald of the Lord, was standing at the gates.

SUGGESTED QUESTIONS FOR STUDY AND DISCUSSION

1. What was the significance of Anna to the redemption brought by Christ?
2. Why was Anna the last prophetess?
3. What was the significance of Anna's ancestry to an acceptance of Jesus as the Christ?

PETER'S MOTHER-IN-LAW

And when Jesus was come into Peter's house, he saw his wife's mother laid, and sick of a fever.

—MATT. 8:14.

READ: MATTHEW 8:14-17

WHEN Jesus said to Peter and Andrew, "Follow me!" they forsook all that they had and followed Him. The ties that had bound had to be severed, and new bonds had to be substituted for these. Peter no longer belonged to Bethsaida, and still less to the family of Jonas. He belonged to Jesus and to His Kingdom. We remember that Jesus said: "He that loveth father or mother more than me is not worthy of me." If ever a demand seemed radically exacting, it was this one. The very thought of it makes us tremble. And yet the early Christians made that sacrifice because of their convictions. They forsook everything, completely everything, their families and their property, in order to follow Jesus.

Just because the demand that everything be forsaken was so exacting, we like to hear now and then that a former bond between a disciple and his family was reconfirmed. We know that that is what happened in the case of Salome, the mother of John and James, and that it happened in this instance between Peter and his mother-in-law. Both of these women, it seems, had been converted to the faith. That is indisputably true of the mother of the sons of Zebedee, and we may take it for granted in the case of Peter's mother-in-law. We may take it for granted because the Lord healed her, and we know that most of the Lord's miracles were perfected where faith had been accomplished.

22

And we know, besides, that this woman worshipped the Lord after the miracle had been performed upon her.

We can not determine exactly whether this woman lived in Bethsaida or in Capernaum. It does not make much difference, for both little places were not separated farther from each other than Chicago is from Evanston. Peter and Andrew owned a house in that village. It had probably represented their father's legacy to them at the time of his death, and the inheritance had never been proportionately divided. Peter was a married man, and when he determined to follow Jesus he could no longer provide for his wife. It seems that he and Andrew together had therefore given her this house, and that she had invited her mother to come to live with her. We do not know whether Andrew was also married, and whether or not any children were born to the marriage of Peter. But we do know that Peter's wife was still living after Paul's public appearance (I Cor. 9:5). Hence, we know that she lived with her mother in Peter's house.

The aged mother-in-law was sick. We have reason to believe that her fever was critically dangerous, for we know that those who attended her were anxious about her. When Jesus came to Peter's house from the synagogue, they immediately told Him of her, and asked Him to assist her. After He had heard that, Jesus immediately went to her bed-chamber. Upon arriving there, Jesus took a position at the head of the bed, stretched out His hand, and touched her temples. By that touch He subdued the high fever, and the woman arose. As a dutiful housewife, she immediately went to the kitchen to make sure that a meal was being prepared for Jesus and His disciples. We read that she arose and ministered unto Him.

There is a spiritual significance in this incident of the Gospel. It arises from the attitude Jesus assumed toward the family of His disciple. The unequivocal command had been that His disciples forsake everything. If Peter had been unwilling to do that he would have been unqualified for the Kingdom of God. That absolute command did not, however, imply that all filial relations were to be severed once and for all. We observe that when the occasion permitted, Peter visited his family again. On this occasion Peter returned with Jesus, and his family joined him in praising his Master and Lord.

But this story interests us also because it comments significantly on a certain domestic relationship. Mothers-in-law are invariably made the objects of continuous ridicule. Wherever that is the case, the husband of the family does all he can to curb the influence of his mother-in-law. And we must admit that many a mother-in-law invites such conduct. In this instance, however, because of the fervent filial love which characterized the families of Israel, and because Jesus' spirit permeated all the members of this family, we observe that the mother-in-law was loved by all. She lived in Peter's house. Now that she had become ill, everyone had joined in praying for her. As for her, this aged woman had not entered that home to rule it or to be served there like a princess. She did the serving herself, and her habit of serving had become so essential a part of her that she could not refrain from doing so even in this thrilling moment. Not that she became "all excited about it." She did not go trotting about the neighborhood, telling everyone that she had been made the object of a miracle. Inasmuch as she had been healed by Jesus, she felt that it was an honor for her to be able to serve Him. She loved and was loved, and for that reason a beautiful harmony existed between her and those about her.

We can all learn from her miraculous recovery that we may ask God to heal our ordinary illnesses as well as such more serious ones as cholera, influenza, or leprosy. He is also willing to cure a common fever. We need not necessarily be suffering from smallpox, from typhoid fever, or from diphtheria to be warranted in asking God for His aid. We must ask our Saviour to help us also when we suffer diseases which do not threaten to take our lives.

Suggested Questions for Study and Discussion

1. What did it mean to the disciples when Christ said, "Follow me"?
2. Did Christ heal this woman entirely?
3. What particular lesson can mothers-in-law and sons-in-law learn from this incident?

SALOME

Then came to him the mother of Zebedee's children, with her sons, worshipping him, and desiring a certain thing of him. —MATT. 20:20.

READ: MATTHEW 20:20-28; MARK 15:40, 41

SALOME was the wife of Zebedee, and was, accordingly, the mother of John and James. One notices this at once by comparing Mark 15:40 with Matthew 27:56. Mark gives us the name of Salome as one of the women who supervised Jesus' burial. In Matthew her name is not given, but she is there designated as the mother of the sons of Zebedee. Salome could, therefore, consider herself a blessed woman, for she was the mother of two of Jesus' best loved disciples. It is indisputable that the three apostles whom Jesus loved most were Peter, John and Paul. The others could not stand in the shadow of these. But before Paul publicly appeared, James occupied the third position in this trio. Together with Peter and John he is always named separately. He disappeared just as Paul was about to take his place, but he died the death of a martyr (Acts 12:2), and because of that his entrance into heaven preceded that of the other apostles. Eleven men had witnessed Jesus' ascension from the Mount of Olives, and of these, James was the first to be called into blessed communion with the glorified Redeemer.

Accordingly, Salome's life was well spent. Her two sons will always retain their honorable position among the group of the Apostles. James was the first to receive the crown of honor, and John was the last to die. But John had the special distinction of being the only one of the apostles to be called to witness the Revelations upon Patmos.

26

Salome was a fisherman's wife. She lived on the coast of the Lake of Genesareth. Her husband, Zebedee, owned boats and nets, and Jesus called her two sons, John and James, as these were busy at assisting their father in mending the nets. Because of that Salome was unexpectedly exalted to an honorable privilege. She could only have hoped to leave her two sons a scow and some nets. Now she suddenly observed that they had taken a position among the apostles to the King, to Whom is given all power in heaven and upon earth. Such sudden change of fortune would induce any mother's ambitions to lose their equilibrium, and would be apt to cause her to have exaggerated expectations.

A legend tells us that Salome was born from Joseph by a first marriage, and attempts in this way to connect her with the family of Mary. Still another legend states that she was a daughter of Zacharias. These legends, at least, tend to bring out this one truth, namely, that James and John, inasmuch as they immediately left their father and their nets, must, in some way, have heard of Jesus before. But that circumstance by no means proves that there was a blood-relationship. It merely indicates that they were related to Jesus in spirit, and for that reason we may conclude that Zebedee's family had also gone to listen to John as he preached at the Jordan. By this means the father, the mother, and the sons were prepared to associate with Jesus. We know, at least, that the two sons immediately agreed to accompany Jesus, and that Zebedee did not try to detain them. Salome, so far from trying to withhold them from Jesus, herself later goes to where the Lord was preaching. She joins the other women. Later, when the Lord has been taken from the Cross, she was one of the women who prepared linen and spices for His burial.

The one sin which is recorded against her is that which she shared with the apostles. She acknowledged that Jesus was the Messiah, but she could not yet segregate that Messiah from Israel's temporal glory. She was what we would call a Millennialist, and did not yet comprehend that not they who are born of Abraham, but they whose faith resembles his, are the seed of Abraham. She noticed that Jesus preferred her sons and Peter to the rest of the apostles, and when she saw that, she eagerly wished that they might retain their position of honor in the Kingdom of Israel that was to be established. It even seems to have irked her somewhat as a mother, that the Lord sometimes seemed to prefer Peter to her own children. These reasons induced her to make the sinful petition of Jesus that He place her two sons on His right and on His left side, respectively, when He should come into His kingdom. That petition arose from maternal pride and maternal jealousy, but it was a sinful prayer all the same. It did not arise from faith, but it opposed faith.

What was Jesus' answer? He asked about whether or not her sons would be prepared to drink of the cup of martyrdom. He seems to say: Indeed, your sons will occupy a distinguished position, but not one such as you imagine. One of your sons will be the first apostolical martyr, and the other will be the last. Let that be their eternal crown!

SUGGESTED QUESTIONS FOR STUDY AND DISCUSSION

1. What sons did Salome contribute to Jesus' first followers?

2. In what rank did these sons stand? What is the order of their death?

3. What was the besetting sin of Salome? Was this due to her pride in her sons?

THE WOMAN WITH AN ISSUE OF BLOOD

*And, behold, a woman, which was diseased with an issue
of blood twelve years, came behind him and touched the
hem of his garment.*

—MATT. 9:20.

READ: MARK 5:25-34

T HE terrible curse of Paradise, "In sorrow thou shalt
bring forth children" has a deeper significance than
the mere actual delivery of the child. It also implies that
some women will have terrible suffering even though no
child-birth actually takes place, and that others will suffer
terribly because of the prolonged consequences of child-
birth. In His independent sovereignty the Lord does not
equally divide the portion of suffering which each woman
is to bear. The quantity of suffering in each woman's cup
varies. Some are compelled to drink only a few, hasty
drops of it. For others it has been filled to the brim. The
suffering of such women is excruciating, be it while they
are delivered or afterwards. It is a suffering made more
intense by the fact that delicacy seems to demand that she
keep much of it a secret.

For that reason it pleases us to notice that the gospel also
includes comfort for those who suffer in this way. It tells
us how a woman who suffered from this secret pain also
came into direct contact with Jesus. That woman's name
is unknown, and has perhaps for refinement's sake been
withheld from us. She is, therefore, generally designated
as the woman "with an issue of blood." She had gone
through a period of intense pain. For twelve long years
nothing had been found which could stop the flow of blood.

29

We are not told whether or not she had retained the disease as the result of child-birth. That makes no difference. The important fact is that she was a woman whose energy had flowed from her, not for months, but for a period of years. Hence, you can imagine how pale, and wan, and haggard she must have looked. And you can get a conception, too, of how energetic her faith must have been. If it had not been so she would not have dared to mingle with the crowd in public.

And yet she did not dare to go to Jesus to talk to Him about it openly. She felt ashamed of herself. Hence, she determined to creep up behind Jesus, and if it should prove possible, to touch the hem of his coat. Because of that act of faith energy passed out of Jesus, and for that reason He noticed it. At once the courageous woman was healed. The blood ceased flowing.

That woman's faith was all the more remarkable, because of the repeated disappointments with which she had met in those many years. First she must have gone to the physicians. That was the perfectly appropriate thing to do, for these are a gift of God to suffering humanity. Whenever we are afflicted by diseases we should gratefully make use of their services. But the gift of medicine, like so many others, is quite imperfect, and frequently becomes distorted because of sin. In the case of this woman, the physicians had not only been unable to help her, but we read, besides, that they caused her much pain, and that her illness became worse at their hands. Perhaps they were not responsible for that. But they were, at least, guilty of robbing her of her means of livelihood, and of depriving her of the means of getting nourishing food for her weakened body. Indeed, it could have been easily understood if this woman had despaired of all hope, and had surrendered herself grumblingly to her fate.

But faith prevented despair from mastering her. A higher grace had accomplished that faith in her heart. Accordingly, she went to Jesus. She did not ask Him for medicine, nor did she burden Him with a long story of her suffering. She went there merely to touch the hem of His garment. Her faith told her that would suffice to heal her. She was right; she returned to her home completely recovered.

Faith can accomplish such stupendous things. Jesus Himself said to her, "Thy faith hath made thee whole." Her faith had not rejected the assistance of physicians simply because these were imperfect and because they were often greedy. Her faith induced her to make use of every gift which God had given for the alleviation of suffering; she left no stone unturned to find grace in God's sight through ordinary means which He had appointed. Because of faith, however, she did not lose hope when medical aid had failed, but kept on extending her hands to the Omnipotence of the Lord. The Mediator rewards such faith not by healing everyone who suffers, but by preventing despair. He rewards it by holding before sufferers a vision of the compassion of our God.

SUGGESTED QUESTIONS FOR STUDY AND DISCUSSION

1. Was the decree of God, "in sorrow thou shalt bring forth children," meant to be intensive for every woman?

2. What trait in this woman led her to touch Jesus' garment?

3. Does God reward the faith of everyone by healing their suffering? If not, what does He do?

MARY MAGDALENE

And certain women, which had been healed of evil spirits
and infirmities, Mary called Magdalene, out of whom went
seven devils.

—LUKE 8:2.

READ: LUKE 8:1-3; MATTHEW 28:1-15

MARY MAGDALENE is Peter's feminine counterpart in the circle which followed Jesus. Both were characterized by much zeal and fervor, and in both that fervor sometimes leaped over its appropriate boundaries; it became impetuosity and had to be punished.

Magdala, Mary's natal town, was situated about three miles from Capernaum. Hence, it is not surprising that she soon heard about Jesus and came into direct contact with Him. That is especially true because she was a conspicuous figure in Magdala. She was a comparatively rich woman, but she had been most cruelly subjected to the influence of devils. Seven devils had made her personality their seat. There are some who infer from this fact that she was an adulterous woman. That is by no means a necessary implication. She had nothing in common with the repentant sinner who washed Jesus' feet. But we may safely infer from the fact that she was possessed of devils that she was by nature very passionate and impetuous. Such persons are most susceptible to the influence of devils, and all such spiritual qualms arise from a sinful condition of the human heart.

But Mary had finally been purged of these influences. She had gone to Jesus. Jesus understood her, because He observed that faith was mingled with her passionate petitions.

Then He became her Saviour and cast seven devils out of her. After that moment, Mary's passionate fervor, just as did Peter's, directed itself to but a single end. She dedicated her life to Jesus as a sacrifice of thanksgiving.

There is a legend about her which says that she went to Rome after Jesus had ascended to heaven, and asked for an interview with the Emperor, in order to indict Pilate for having made a false judgment in Jesus' trial. This cannot be true for it would imply opposition to the faith in the Cross. But it, at least, points out what was characteristic in Mary Magdalene's character.

She constantly remained with the women who followed Jesus and His disciples, and who served Him with the necessaries they had taken with them. Such ministrations represented Divine care for Jesus as long as He remained upon earth. Naturally, He and His disciples needed money for food, shelter, and clothing. That money was provided by these women, and, as one of these, Mary Magdalene was also permitted to give her entire treasure to the Lord.

But that is not the only token of her attachment to the Saviour. When Jesus went up to Jerusalem "to suffer many things, and to be put to death," Mary Magdalene accompanied Him. At the Cross all of the disciples except John, but including Peter, fled from Him in His suffering. But Mary Magdalene displayed sufficient feminine resilience to be able to witness the death of the Mediator (Mark 15:40, 41). And after the events upon Golgotha had occurred, she remained equally faithful to her Redeemer. She, too, participated in the preparations for the burial. She was one of the women who went to the sepulcher at dawn to scatter spices in the grave. And when they found that the body was not there, it was Mary Magdalene who at once went to Jerusalem to find Peter, and to tell him that the corpse had been stolen.

Even then she was not content. She was a constantly
active and a very ready woman. She immediately returned
to the grave, most likely even before the Apostles had
arrived there, in order to keep abreast of what was going
on. We know that Jesus met her then, that she did not
recognize Him (how typically characteristic of such impetuous natures!), but that she was nevertheless the first woman
to see Him. Her eyes revealed nothing to her. She had to
be spoken to, and her name had to be called before her
spiritual eyes were opened. Then she recognized Him, and
acknowledged Him by falling upon her knees. Then, too,
the Lord had to rebuke her zealous impetuosity. She was
not to touch Him. Her too aggressive fervor, her impetu-
ousness had to be tempered, or she would have been con-
sumed by it. Not every woman of Jesus' circle was as
passionate as that. Mary of Nazareth was different, Salome
was very different from that, and so was Martha, Lazarus'
sister.

But a fervent nature, and the zeal of feminine ardor had
to be represented in that group of women. It was represented in those good things she did, but it was also represented in her undue impetuosity. It was represented in her,
in order that our Saviour could be refreshed by such ardor
and in order that He could temper an exaggeration of it.
The situation in Jesus' Church is no different from what it
was in His little circle. The Church may not snub the
Magdalenes.

SUGGESTED QUESTIONS FOR STUDY AND DISCUSSION

1. Of whom, among Jesus' apostles, is she the counterpart? Why?

2. What was the weakness in Mary Magdalene's character?

3. In what especial way did she help Jesus?

MARY, THE MOTHER OF THE APOSTLE

Now there stood by the cross of Jesus his mother, and his mother's sister, Mary the wife of Cleophas, and Mary Magdalene.

—JOHN 19:25.

READ: JOHN 19:25-42

WE must guard against confusing the six Marys of whom we are told in the New Testament. These are: (1) Mary of Nazareth, the mother of the Lord; (2) Mary of Bethany, the sister of Lazarus; (3) Mary of Magdala; (4) Mary of Jerusalem, the mother of John Mark; (5) Mary of Rome, an aide to Paul; and (6) Mary, the mother of the Apostle, whose home we do not know, although we are told she stayed in the neighborhood of the Lake of Galilee.

At this point we shall speak only of the last-named Mary, who is best distinguished from the others by the name of "the mother of the apostle." She is sometimes called "the other Mary," but that is a name which signified nothing and leads to confusion.

She had married Cleophas of Alpheus and had borne him two sons, James and Joses. Jesus chose the first of these as one of His apostles. For purposes of differentiating between him and the brother of John, he is generally designated James "the Less." But these are all of the particulars that we know about her. Whatever else can be related concerning her can as well be said of all the women who followed Jesus. She followed Jesus, and ministered to Him with her goods. She witnessed the spectacle of the Cross; she participated in Jesus' burial; and she was one of those

35

who first heard that Immanuel had arisen from the grave. To this extent she is equal to Joanna, the wife of Chuza the steward, and to Susanna, and to other prominent women who had this in common, that they loved the Lord, and served Him unobtrusively.

If we should compare this Mary with Mary Magdalene by an analogy to our two types of letters, we should be inclined to call Mary Magdalene a vowel and Mary, the mother of the apostle, a consonant. The same analogy holds if we compare Peter with James the Less. We should then name Peter, who always took the initiative, the vowel, and James, who always remained in the background, the consonant. This Mary and those other quiet women were very much like James. They were consonants, they harmoniously joined in with the song of love that was sung for Jesus, but they were not originally creative. The world generally looks askance at such quiet service. To be very ordinary, to be in no way extraordinary, to always assist others in quiet and unobtrusive service, it is thought, is too tame and too unambitious an attitude to assume.

But God's scale of values weighs differently than ours does. In our alphabet, God gave us five vowels and twenty-one consonants. And He has given the human race very few people who are to assume solo parts. To the many others He has granted only the capacity to harmonize when others lead in creation's hymn of love and praise. That situation is quite appropriate. Only in that way can a supreme harmony be attained. A company of successive soloists would be repulsive to our æsthetic sense.

In this sense it cannot be said that a rich gospel did not proceed from Mary. Those who hear of a Peter, a Paul, or a John know that the ambitions of these exceed their capacities. They are simply unequal to the task of such

heroes. Very few feel that they are on a par with Mary
Magdalene. For that reason it is expedient for ministers
of the Word to constantly place such characters in the
foreground.

Mary, the mother of the apostle, reared a child for the
service of the Lord. After that she inconspicuously and
unobtrusively served Jesus. She was motivated by the inner
urge of a sincere love. She sacrificed her substance to her
Lord. As we contemplate her, we feel that thousands, and
again thousands of women in the Church of Christ will
feel at home with her. They seem to recognize their own
position in that which she occupied. They are attracted to
her and feel inspired to more arduous zeal because of her
example.

God appointed man to be more aggressively active than
that. But the function of a consonant, that of "joining in
the chorus," is a very natural and appropriate function for
a woman. If that does not satisfy you as a woman, then,
in the profoundest recesses of your heart some rebellious
sin is lodged. That sin will constantly tempt you to emu-
late the world, and will make of you a Dinah, who went out
to visit the daughters of the land. But you can transcend
that temptation. The quiet faith can beckon as effectively
as that which is spectacular. If it can do that for you, the
position which this less prominent Mary occupied in life
will have a sacred charm for you. Then it will be a great
tribute if it can be said of you after you have died: "She
loved Jesus, and she served her Saviour unobtrusively."

SUGGESTED QUESTIONS FOR STUDY AND DISCUSSION
1. Identify the six Marys of the New Testament.
2. What is the charm in the life of this Mary?
3. What was the significance of her example to the
   Christian women of her time?

MARY OF BETHANY

But one thing is needful: and Mary hath chosen that
good part, which shall not be taken away from her.
—LUKE 10:42.

READ: LUKE 10:38-42; JOHN 12:1-9

MARY OF BETHANY represents a woman of mysticism in contrast with Martha who represents a woman of pietism. There is an external world which surrounds us, but there is another world which is concealed within our hearts. Because of this fact every woman can choose to do one of two things. She can choose to use the inner world as a chamber of resources with which to beautify the world outside of her, or she can retreat from the external world and take refuge in the world within her. These two formulations, of course, represent two extremes, and between them all kinds of medial positions can be taken. But the primary contrast, nevertheless, remains. One woman feels an urge to go out into the world, while another chooses to live in her own seclusion. If the active woman who wishes to be busy in the external world is a Christian, she will become a pietist, and will devote herself to all kinds of Christian philanthropy. On the other hand, her counterpart, who prefers to recede into herself, will, if she chooses for Christ, surrender herself to the sweetness and beauty of mystical meditation.

Which of these tendencies will dominate in you is less a matter of deliberate choice than of temperamental and instinctive predilections, as they are affected by the environment. Because of that you must beware of a too one-sided decision: the pietistic woman may not pass judgment upon her mystical sister, and the mystical personality may not look down with disdain upon her pietistic acquaintance.

Both types of characters have a right to exist. We cannot get along without either. A world in which only aggressive women could be found would soon be wanting in intense and profound thoughts and meditations. And, if all women were introspective and pensive, life would soon become little more than a dream.

For that reason Mary of Bethany also occupied her own peculiar position in Jesus' group of friends. She represents a woman who had cultivated profound inner thoughts. She was busier internally than she was externally. She saw what others did not see. She quietly observed everything. By such constant introspection she has learned that there is such a thing as an internal world. This inner world charmed her, and she constantly found herself sinking into it.

The three remarkable particulars which we are told concerning her all betray that she was this kind of woman. A year before the events involving Lazarus, Jesus had stopped at her home in Bethany. On that occasion Martha hastened to serve Jesus. But Mary placed herself quietly and peacefully at His feet, and became lost in His heavenly discourse. A year later Lazarus died. We observe that Martha had already run to meet Jesus, when Mary was still too dazed by the event and too occupied with grief to know what was going on about her. Not long after that Jesus was about to go to the cross, and was again stopping at Bethany. Martha had prepared the meal and had made it a point that nothing should be lacking at the table. But Mary felt that something was still wanting. She mingled Divine poetry with the prose of the situation by anointing Jesus with a bottle of expensive spikenard. Thus she seemed to want to dedicate the Lamb of God to the sacrifice He was about to make.

These finer, more delicate, more spiritual personalities usually meet less sympathy in the world than do their more aggressive opposites. That is even true among Christians. That is perfectly natural, for pietism can point to more demonstrable results. Pietism is always active, and in this way it accomplishes many good works. And yet it is worth commenting upon that Mary appealed to Jesus more strongly than did Martha. He defended Mary against the criticism of her sister. At the grave of Lazarus, Mary's tears affected Him more touching than Martha's did. And when the spikenard was poured over His sacred head, Jesus assured Mary that she would be remembered throughout the coming generations.

We may not, of course, misuse this opinion of Jesus by an attempt to justify a sickly, sentimental mysticism. We may not use it to argue that sheer passiveness is as virtuous as practical activity. There was nothing sickly or maudlin in Mary's mysticism. And we know that Jesus also praised Martha.

Nevertheless, we are warned by the example of Mary of Bethany not to ignore the value of emotional life, and not to under-estimate the worth of a life spent in meditating on God. Some provide the oil for the lamps in God's church, and others light those lamps. Without saying that we can get along without someone to light these lamps, it, nevertheless, remains true that the oil in them is "the one thing needful." If only the oil is there, the hand that lights will certainly be provided.

SUGGESTED QUESTIONS FOR STUDY AND DISCUSSION

1. What was the good part that Mary chose?
2. How did she dedicate Christ to His sacrifice? What other things are recorded of her?
3. Is a purely sentimental mysticism ever justified?

MARTHA

But Martha was cumbered about much serving and came to him and said, Lord, dost thou not care that my sister hath left me to serve alone? bid her therefore that she help me.

—LUKE 10:40.

READ: JOHN 11:1-45

FOR some reason or another, Martha's reputation does not stand particularly high among Christians. It is impossible for us to talk about Martha without thinking at the same time about her sister Mary. And these two are about as different as light is from darkness. Mary was a quiet, pious Christian who enjoyed the peace of listening to His conversation as she sat at Jesus' feet. Martha was her active and industrious sister. She was always busy at dusting, straightening out the rooms, serving refreshments, and preparing the meals. And yet, whoever thinks that Martha's relation to Mary was that of darkness to light, respectively, thinks so without Scriptural warrant.

It is true that Mary was the better woman. In the Church of Christ some busy themselves with silver, others with gold, and still others with mere wood and stone. Using that apostolical measure we can say that the difference between Mary and Martha is that the former worked in gold and the latter in silver. We must grant that such a distinction can be conceded to Mary. But we would be interpreting the Apostle's figure very incorrectly if we supposed that all are to work in gold, and that he who works in silver is not doing his duty. God's sovereign election should be taken into account in this matter. He called one to be an Isaiah and another to be an

41

Amos. But Amos must be himself and not Isaiah. John was an Evangelist who worked in pure gold, but Mark would have shirked his responsibility if he had neglected to work in silver, and had vainly attempted to imitate John. The same relationship holds in this instance. God had placed two sisters in Lazarus' family, had given each her appropriate talents, and accordingly, had given to each a peculiar calling. For that reason each acquitted herself of her responsibility only when she followed her own particular path.

It will not do to answer in response to these arguments that Jesus reprimanded Martha. It is true that He reprimanded her, but pay close attention to the reason for it. When Mary was paying rapt attention to Jesus' conversation, Martha busied herself about domestic duties. Jesus did not reprimand her for doing that. He did not tell her, "Do as Mary does." Not a word is said about that. But when Martha valued her own silver more highly than Mary's gold, when she told Jesus, "Tell Mary to assist me in serving," then Jesus felt that she had to be enlightened. How could He have done anything else? Then He had to tell her that Mary had not chosen to do the less desirable, but the more desirable thing.

In her restless activity, Martha looked down with disdain upon her sister's quiet, peaceful, faith-engendered mysticism. She had no right to do that. Gold had to be valued as gold, even by those to whom God had given silver. The parallelism between these two women and the ministry of the Word as compared with that of mercy is striking. At present there are many in God's church who are busily engaged in services of mercy. Such occupations are highly desirable. There is always a great need for such services, and God has commanded us to engage in them. But suppose, now, that a Christian who was always active in such pursuits, should look askance at the Service of the Word. Suppose he should conclude that it would be much more beneficial for the Kingdom, if the minister should devote his time as a deacon would, by ministering to the needy. Surely, such a man would be inviting the reprimand: "Only one thing is needful, and whoever makes the Word his fortress, has chosen the better part." He who engages in works of mercy is working in silver, and he who ministers the Word is working in gold.

Martha was, therefore, proud of her own particular work, and that undue pride was a sin. Apart from that, however, Martha was a believing woman who was characterized by true integrity. She ardently loved her Lord and shared His confidence. This is a richly significant fact. Many women in our families are necessarily so busily occupied with menial cares that they have scarcely any time to work in gold. But to be occupied in this way is also to be busy in the service of God, and such women have many reasons to be grateful for the portion of grace which has been allotted to them.

When the conversation between Mary and Jesus had ended, they both sat down to the meal which Martha had prepared. In this way Martha, too, served her Lord and Saviour, even though her service was of a lower order than that of Mary.

Suggested Questions for Study and Discussion

1. Are we justified in having a low estimation of the value of Martha to her Lord?
2. What is the rank of Martha compared with that of her sister Mary?
3. Is there a place in Christ's Church for the Marthas? If so, why?

THE WOMAN OF SAMARIA

*There cometh a woman of Samaria to draw water: Jesus
saith unto her, Give me to drink.*

—JOHN 4:7.

READ JOHN 4:1-42

NOTHING induces us to question our usual notices of
Christian propriety so much as does the spiritual
and devoted care which Jesus bestowed upon the Samari-
tan woman of Sychar. If that woman had lived in one
of our localities she would scarcely have been noticed.
In the first place, the fact that this woman had already
been married five times does not make a favorable impression upon us. There is no reason to censure a widow
for marrying a second time. She can even marry twice
after her first husband's death without exciting suspicion.
Perhaps it would even be possible a third time. But we
certainly can not get ourselves to praise her for having
married five times before she had become very old. We
can, of course, make a more serious indictment against
her character than that. She was not even satisfied after
she had buried her fifth husband. And inasmuch as no
proposal of marriage was offered her at this time, she had
simply determined to live with a man without the
formality of a wedding.

We notice, besides, that she certainly was an independent and bold woman. We can hear it in the intona-
tions of her voice, and we can see it in her manner of
going about among the inhabitants of Sychar. On the
whole, we get the impression that she was altogether

too bold, and that her forwardness sometimes was positively uncouth. She was a ready woman, one never embarrassed, always knew what to say, and had grown
calloused to appropriate feminine modesty. Doubtless,
we should feel inclined to avoid such a woman if she
lived in our locality. We would not care to associate
with her, would not care to be seen with her in public.

And yet God's Providence directed matters in such a
way that this superficial, mundane, and gullible woman
enjoyed an experience which the noblest of women can
not avoid envying her for. This experience did not occur
to her accidentally. It was not a situation in which
Jesus did not know to whom He was talking. Jesus knew
perfectly well that she had been living immorally. He
could, therefore, have filled her vessel and have let her
depart with it, without having spoken to her. But Jesus
did not do that. He began a conversation with her, and
apparently did so intentionally, for He at once gave a
symbolically spiritual significance to His words.

At first this woman could not understand what He
meant. Gullible women are generally superficial. But
Jesus persisted; He would not let her go. He gradually
made the thrust of His words penetrate her heart and her
conscience more deeply. After that He did not send her
away with the warning that she should no longer live in
adultery. Instead, He revealed rich secrets to her, first
about the worship of the Father, and, secondly, about
His own Messianic mission. Some of the profoundest
revelations which Jesus ever made were given to this
woman. That fact is especially striking if we remember
that there must have been many gentle, pious women in
Israel at that time. But Jesus passed by these in order

to give this bold woman of Sychar the privilege of a significant interview.

In fact, the incident seemed so unplausible to many that exactly because of the strangeness of it, they called the woman's story a fiction. Naturally, to do so displayed unthoughtful criticism. Such an uncouth woman would be most unlikely to see such delicate, spiritual visions. In fact, no poet could have created such a vision. That fact makes us surer that this narrative represents the truth and that it can have a rich significance for us. The content of Jesus' conversation is not the only significant aspect of this entire incident. The whole event teaches us something about social relationships, and about the false conception of our own piety which we may sometimes have. We should have avoided and ignored a person such as the woman of Samaria was, in the belief that her condition was irretrievably hopeless anyway. And Jesus selected her to be converted to the faith, and induced her to make a confession of Him.

Besides, this incident reprimands us for sometimes vainly believing that we are noble and good. Surely, the Saviour (we argue at such times) will refuse to have any relations with a woman like that! But He will come to us, to a pious, virtuous woman. Such attitudes resemble that of which we read in the Scriptures: "Depart from me, for I am holier than thou." The account of the woman of Samaria makes us ashamed of all such deliberations. The grace of Election always remains sovereign and independent. Divine grace seeks the lost, not those who are righteous. The whole matter is simply a question of whether or not the conscience can be touched. Thank God, that that was still possible in the case of the woman of Samaria.

SUGGESTED QUESTIONS FOR STUDY AND DISCUSSION

1. What was the general character of this woman of Samaria?

2. What is the significance to us of Jesus' conversation with her?

3. What attitude does Christ's treatment of this woman teach us to take toward those outside the church? Do we always do it?

THE WOMAN OF CANAAN

And, behold, a woman of Canaan came out of the same coasts, and cried unto him, saying, Have mercy on me, O Lord, thou son of David! My daughter is grievously vexed with a devil.

—MATT. 15:22.

READ: MATTHEW 15:21-28; MARK 7:24-30

WAS the woman of Canaan a converted woman? Was the extraordinary faith which Jesus praised in her the true, saving faith? The narrative does not answer these questions. We are told only that she believed Jesus' power to work miracles and that she insisted unquestioningly in petitioning Him, until her child had shared in the benefits of that power. Hence, her faith was like that of which Jesus spoke when He said: "If ye have faith as a grain of mustard seed ye shall say unto this mountain, Remove hence to yonder place; and it shall remove." We read besides that there will be bread for the children, and crumbs for the dogs. That bread refers to the power of miracles with which Jesus blessed Israel, and those crumbs refer to the same power which the woman of Canaan hoped would be used in her daughter's favor.

For that reason this narrative tells us nothing about the influence of spiritual grace. That she was by no means a regenerated woman becomes perfectly obvious from the fact that Jesus included her among the "dogs" who represented the heathens. This does not mean to say that she did not later become converted as the result of Jesus' miracle. The important matter is that

48

in this narrative she appears not as a believing or converted woman, but as a heathen, who had an unusually strong faith in Jesus' capacity for perfecting miracles.

Such "faith in the miraculous" is far inferior in quality to the true "saving faith," for it can not redeem the soul. At the same time, however, we must remember that that first kind of faith is also a precious gift of God's grace. Such faith does not imply an appreciation of our sin and misery, and for that reason it does not result in a need for salvation. But it has at least this desirable characteristic to boast of. It clings to the conviction that spirit dominates matter. So far from completely surrendering itself to human assistance, it reaches for a saving power which transcends that.

She was not only a pagan woman, but a descendant from the old, sinful Canaanites. Israel had once driven them out of their country, and after that the people of Canaan had made Phoenicia their home. Accordingly, her background was against her. She lived within the boundaries of Tyre and Sidon, and the reputation of these cities was extremely low.

Exactly because of her unfavorable environment, we are sure that this woman's faith in the miraculous was not the product of her natural tendencies, but that it indisputably was the result of the common grace of God. The Lord God was glorified by arranging the meeting between this woman and His beloved Son. Because of the interview and the miracle which ensued upon the woman's unusual faith, God embarrassed Israel and glorified Himself. The contrast between Israel and this woman is a striking one. Hence, it has always been pleasantly supposed that she clung to the Messiah, even though it occurred largely by an external attachment. It is thought that this woman's conscience shrieked to Jesus to protest against Israel's proud belief that God's grace should forever be limited to one nation.

If you care to ask upon what the faith in the miraculous depends, the answer is that it does not rest upon that grace of God which delivers men from sin, but that it depends upon His omnipotence and upon the Divine compassion which delivers men from human misery. And if you should care to ask, besides, to what methods such faith resorts, the answer must be that it perseveres in prayer. This woman teaches that one thing: In every distress we must pray. The woman of Canaan prayed intelligently, she knew that Jesus could save her daughter. She prayed relentlessly, and because she persevered, she triumphed.

It is true that she did not pray for a spiritual blessing, either for herself or for her daughter. In spite of that, however, she teaches us what the mystery of prayer is like. It is a prayer in which there is not the faintest suggestion of doubt. The woman of Canaan illustrated that she was quite willing to completely surrender herself to God's independent sovereignty. Her prayer became more passionate and more ardent the longer the answer was delayed and withheld. Because of that her prayer was one which was later answered. James speaks of the hesitating person in prayer as being similar to a "wave of the sea driven with the wind and tossed." The woman of Canaan illustrated exactly the opposite. She illustrated, besides, how rich the gift of faith is, that can be accomplished in the heart of an unbeliever. It is a glorious gift, even though it differs essentially from the true and genuine faith which is given to God's elect as the means of salvation.

SUGGESTED QUESTIONS FOR STUDY AND DISCUSSION

1. What does the statement "there will be bread for the children, and crumbs for the dogs" refer to?

2. Does God sometimes put us to shame, by exemplifying to us the heathen's "faith in the miraculous"? How?

3. What does this woman teach us, as to prayer, and perseverance?

PILATE'S WIFE

When he was set down on the judgment seat, his wife sent unto him, saying, Have thou nothing to do with that just man: for I have suffered many things this day in a dream because of him.

—MATT. 27:19.

READ: MATTHEW 27:15-31

IT sometimes happens that a harsh and austere man is blessed with a wife whose gentler emotional life exerts a beneficial and saving influence upon him. This was true in the case of Pilate. He is depicted by history as a tyrannical despot, who respected only brute force and power. We are told that he so frequently abused the people of Jerusalem and Samaria that his superiors were compelled to call him to order. His statement to Jesus, "Knowest thou not that I have power to crucify thee, and have power to release thee?" is a typical expression of the tyrant in him. And this decision to whip and to crucify Jesus after the Lord's innocence had become perfectly clear, is another illustration of his essentially despotical nature.

But God had given this tyrant a wife whose nature was much tenderer and gentler. Besides, she was a wife who knew that it was her duty to temper her husband's violence at every appropriate occasion. We learn from Matthew's account of the gospel that she took an interest in what her husband was doing, that she sympathetically and appreciatively helped him in his official duties, and that she observed his deliberations each time he was confronted by a difficult decision.

In this instance, too, she is not disinterested in Jesus' trial before Pilate. She did more than to merely ask how things went as her husband came in at night. She was genuinely interested in the trial, she had apparently asked who this man Jesus was, and when she learned that He was in no way guilty, she feared that her husband would commit an offense against Him. She fell asleep, filled with such fears. When she awakened she knew that she had dreamed, and that her dream had caused intense anxiety. For she tells us that "she suffered many things" because of Jesus during the night. There is little value in speculating about what kind of dream she dreamed. And it would, perhaps, be of little value to determine definitely whether God directly influenced her by means of that dream. That is entirely possible, but it is by no means certain. We read nothing about it.

Hence, we must limit our thoughts and comments to what we find written about the matter. We may safely infer, then, that this woman retained the same fears by night which she entertained during the day. Such phenomena are quite common to sensitively emotional people. We may safely infer that all kinds of anxious presentiments struck fear in her heart. In her dreams these fears had become personified and had played about her pillow in a thousand shapes and figures. And it can also be definitely said that she awoke to two firm convictions. The first was that Jesus was an innocent Man. And the second was that Pilate would certainly be inviting disaster, if, by reason of his authority, he should unjustly offend that Rabbi.

We do not deny that each of these events took place because God had so directed them. In fact, we firmly believe that He did. It was another means which God had chosen to illustrate that the Man of Sorrows was indeed an innocent man. But Pilate's wife is worth observing merely as the wife of Pilate. Observing her merely as such, we are sure that she displayed true feminine gentleness and care in trying to restrain her husband from committing an atrocity which would be sure to incite God's wrath.

Because of that, this pagan woman should cause many a Christian woman to feel ashamed of herself. She sensed her responsibility to her husband, in spite of the fact that he was by no means an amiable figure. At the same time many Christian wives live on indifferently, as though any conception of responsibility to their husbands had never entered their minds.

The influence which a wife and a husband can mutually exert upon each other cannot be over-estimated. Inasmuch as a woman's chief virtue is the gentleness of her emotional life, she is simply denying her capacities when she refuses to exercise a blessed influence upon her husband. However, Pilate serves as well to admonish many Christian husbands. Angels no longer visit the earth. But God has given many a man a guardian angel in the form of a gentle but profound woman. Wherever that is the case, she serves to restrain him from acts of evil, and to induce him to pursue less drastic ambitions. And we all feel that Pilate added immeasurably to his guilt by failing to profit from his wife's better suggestions. Husbands still are constantly reacting to the influences of their wives in the same way that Pilate did. Whoever callouses himself to the blessed, saving influence of a wife, not only remains as he is, but increases the evil in his heart.

SUGGESTED QUESTIONS FOR STUDY AND DISCUSSION

1. What type of character was Pilate, as a husband, and a ruler?

2. Was his wife a true helpmate to her husband? Why?

3. What can Christian women learn from this meditation? What should men?

HERODIAS

And she went forth, and said unto her mother, What shall I ask? And she said, The head of John the Baptist.
—MARK 6:24.

READ: MARK 6:14-21

HERODIAS was not a native Israelite. She came from Edom, and we know that the blood of Esau coursed in the veins of Herod's whole family. The moral tone of this royal family was of the lowest possible order, and Herodias herself was a very faithful representative of the family in this respect. She was married, and Herod was married, but she had rejected her husband, and Herod his wife, in order that they two could live together in adultery. Her real husband was Philip. He was really a prince, but inasmuch as his father had disowned him, he had been forced to live as an ordinary citizen. Once, when Herod had visited Rome, he had stayed at the home of Philip and Herodias, and on that occasion Herod and Herodias illegitimately fostered love between them. As a result Philip was rewarded for his hospitality by his royal brother's abduction of his wife. Of course, Herod's own wife, a princess of Arabia, constituted an obstacle in the way of this illegitimate marriage. But Herodias skillfully persuaded Herod to divorce her, and to let her, Herodias, reign as queen instead.

Things happened in exactly that way. Herod rejected his own wife. Amid great festivities Herodias entered the King's palace as a queen even before Philip had died. In this way her daughter, Princess Salome, she

56

who could dance so beautifully, also came to the capital.

In this way, too, the spirit of Edom began to permeate God's people more and more. The people of Edom, who had themselves disclaimed a traditional humility, brought all kinds of immoral influences to bear upon the life at the court. And what made the situation worse was the circumstance that all this sin and evil was camouflaged by the luster and glamour of the courtly life.

We know of only one man who had the courage to set the sinfulness which prevailed in that court in its proper light. John the Baptist told Herod without mincing his words that the wife he had married was the wife of his brother and that he, therefore, had no right to have her in his palace. It happened that Herod was a man who was very susceptible to sensuous love. He was not purposefully wicked, and for that reason, although John's words annoyed him, he did not dare to oppose them positively. In fact, he tried to favor John in other respects in an attempt to compensate for his clandestine relations with Herodias.

But Herodias' character was essentially different. She wanted to play the role of a queen. Hence, she had rejected her husband because of his mean social and political status, and had pushed Herod's Arabian princess out of the way. She literally hated the accuser who had placed Herod's conscience in turmoil. Who knows, she questioned herself, that Herod will not listen too closely to John's advice? And if that should be the case, who could assure her that she should remain the queen?

Herodias was also a sensualistic person, but her sensuousness served her pride. Her primary sin was her pride, and her wanton tendencies only served to give expression to her proud ambitions. Pride always hates.

Accordingly, she began to concoct all kinds of murderous schemes. She reasoned that her permanence as a queen would be certain only if John were put to death.

She knew Herod very well. She knew how easily he succumbed to sensual excitement, and that fact started her thinking. And, inasmuch as she felt that she had perhaps lost some of her former charm by this time, she determined to use her daughter, Salome, to incite his passions. In this way she accomplished her foul designs, and, as a result, John was beheaded.

Such conduct induces us to ask with Vondel: "What can not foul ambition foment?" It seems to add to the repulsiveness of it, that it was a woman, not a man, who perpetrated this brutal, insidious plan. Herodias was to Herod what Jezebel was to Ahab. In both instances the man was wicked, and in both instances the woman was more wicked. And in both instances the wife went farther in hate, went farther in bitter, deadly hate against a prophet of God. Jezebel hated Elijah; and Herodias hated John, the Elijah of the New Testament.

A woman's heart when it determines evil can still be that wicked. When she chooses to do good, she blesses more than ever a man can. But the moment she surrenders to sin, her hatred toward the men of God is much more passionate, much fiercer, much more fatal. She will stop at nothing then. Think of it! This woman used her own daughter to excite the sensuous passions of her husband, and then she asked her child to ask that the head of a messenger of God be given her as a gift! Such wickedness is still possible. You can trace a woman's influence in every circle and in every group. You will observe that her influence is active wherever hatred is being fostered against God and His faithful representatives. She may not stand in the foreground, but, if you will observe closely, you will detect that she is exerting a real, if secret influence. In short, this is just another instance in which Eve is conspiring with Satan to induce her husband to oppose God.

SUGGESTED QUESTIONS FOR STUDY AND DISCUSSION

1. What was the first evil act of Herod and Herodias?
2. What evil acts did the latter accomplish through her daughter?
3. What was the sin that brought Herodias to commit these things? Can God accept such as she, who remain unrepentant?

THE PENITENT SINNER

*And behold, a woman in the city, which was a sinner,
when she knew that Jesus sat at meat in the Pharisee's
house, brought an alabaster box of ointment.*
—LUKE 7:37.

READ: LUKE 7:36-50

Anointing was a rather common form of greeting in
Israel. The more prominent Rabbis sometimes
resorted to kissing the feet as another method of greeting
each other. For that reason it is not surprising to find
that Jesus was also welcomed at times by these same
means. It may be that Jesus was frequently anointed
but we know with certainty that he was twice greeted
in that way. This instance in connection with the penitent sinner was the first time, and the second occurred
shortly before His capture. These two instances and
occasions must not be confused. We have no right to
say that this penitent sinner was Mary Magdalene, for
we have not the slightest reason to believe that she was
a public woman.

The penitent sinner of whom we are told in this account was a public woman. She had perhaps carried
on her illicit practices at Nain. There everyone thought
of her as "the sinner." As such she was a despised
figure. She had rejected her virtue and her honor, and
had become guilty of the lowest sin into which a woman
can fall. She sacrificed her body for the gold of any
who chose to come.

Jesus' effective words had induced this woman to stop
and take thought. She suffered qualms of remorse be-

cause of the licentious life she had led. She refrained from her intensely wicked practices. She came to the house of Simon the Pharisee, a prominent lord at whose table Jesus was dining. She fell down at His feet, moistened them with her tears, dried them with her hair, kissed them and anointed them with ointment from an alabaster box.

Accordingly, we read nothing about a bottle of spikenard in this narrative, nothing about breaking the bottle, or about pouring the contents over Jesus' head. This woman merely moistened, dried, kissed and anointed Jesus' feet, and she anointed these with an ointment taken out of an alabaster box. Most likely it was an ointment which she had retained from her former sinful life, inasmuch as we know that such public women misused the perfume of such ointments in their sinful practices.

Here again, we are confronted by the same mystery to which Jesus gave the most striking expression when He said to the lords and ladies of Jerusalem: "The publicans and the harlots go into the kingdom of God before you." This woman, too, had literally been a harlot. And yet the honorable Simon was rejected and she was accepted because she loved Him more. Jesus explained her greater love by the fact that she had been forgiven much more because she had sinned more. That concept seems to us to be a most precarious one, and yet we must accept our Saviour's judgment in the matter. Jesus spoke the truth. The degenerated woman who was despised by the whole city, was far exalted above Simon, the universally respected citizen.

This woman's anointing of Jesus' feet, and what Jesus said in this connection, does throw some light on the nature of this mystery, however. Obviously this woman had a very sympathetic and fervent character. She was not a stoically austere woman. She could not restrain her tears. She moistened Jesus' feet with them. She loosened her hair and dried the tears with it. She pressed one kiss after another upon Jesus' feet. And she did not feel satisfied until the perfume of her ointment arose from Jesus' feet. In His comments, Jesus emphasized these things. He appreciated her warm love, and her fervent sympathy, because these contrasted so strikingly with the calculated, measured coolness of the honorable Simon, a man who could never unbend himself.

The penitent sinner's character was such that it would naturally be very susceptible to the temptation of sensual sins. Sympathy can be a holy thing, but it can also be sinful, and it is that sinful sympathy which causes the degeneration of a harlot. Women who have an austere and somewhat stoical temperament are far less liable to the shame of rejecting their own honor and pride.

Sometimes God's Omnipotence seizes such a sympathetic nature. He purges her ardent sympathy, and makes it pure and holy. And because such persons have not hardened themselves against the influences of grace, the sympathy of faith and of love develops easily and spontaneously in them.

In this way the Lord God humiliates every creature, in order that He alone remain the High and Exalted One. He tells us that He selects His own from all types of sinners, even from the most sinful of creatures. Thus He tells us, too, that if we are chosen, we are chosen only as one sinner among others.

SUGGESTED QUESTIONS FOR STUDY AND DISCUSSION

1. Why is this woman referred to as "a sinner"?
2. How did she reveal her love for Christ? How, in turn, did Christ accept her as a penitent?
3. What does this incident reveal to us, as sinners?

CAIAPHAS' MAID-SERVANT

Now Peter sat without in the palace; and a damsel came unto him, saying, Thou also wast with Jesus of Galilee.
—MATT. 26:69.

READ: MATTHEW 26:56-75

ALTHOUGH we are not given their names, we are told about two maid-servants in the retinue of Caiaphas the high priest. Surely, it is not a mere coincidence that we are told almost the same thing about each of them. We read about the first of these that when she saw Peter standing in the vestibule, she thought it rather entertaining to tease him by saying that he, too, was one of Jesus' disciples. And immediately after that we read that when Peter had gone to another part of the vestibule, another maid-servant did exactly the same thing. These two damsels did not do so by previous agreement. One of them was not merely imitating the other. They did so because they had developed the habit of misusing their position.

Be sure to get a right conception of the situation. It was still deep night. The cock had not yet crowed. Everyone in the neighborhood knew that something especially significant was brewing. Why, otherwise, would everyone be in such a state of excitement and turmoil at this early hour, and why, indeed, had all the members of the Sanhedrin been summoned in the middle of the night?

The high priest's maid-servants had not gone to bed but had been told to keep the fires burning in the grates of the vestibule. Accordingly, these also knew that Jesus was not an ordinary prisoner, and that the death penalty was involved in the trial. For that reason they could readily guess that Peter would dislike nothing so much as to be detected as a disciple of Jesus. They could understand very well that this love for and attachment to Jesus had induced him to enter the vestibule. Doubtless, Peter had changed his dress somewhat, very likely he kept his face half-concealed, and tried to hide himself behind others. But, just because of his reticent behavior, a woman's eye could easily penetrate his disguise, and observe that he was Peter. These two maid-servants did, and, instead of respecting him for his attachment to Jesus, and instead of trying to avert any embarrassment on his part because of mere human sympathy, both took delight in teasing, betraying, and in pointing out in Peter just that which he wished most to conceal. The words of both tore at his heart like the thrust of a dagger.

Their wicked teasing was followed by detrimental results. Their chiding language induced the Apostle of the Lord to commit one of the most grievous sins of his life. Because of it he denied his Saviour. Because of the words of those damsels he cursed his Lord. May we suppose that those maid-servants had intended that their fun should issue in such disastrous consequences? Hardly. They merely wanted to have their fun. They wanted to be interesting, and boldness always seems to succeed in that. They simply entertained themselves at the cost of another's embarrassment.

Because they happened to be engaged in serving a prominent house they supposed that some of that prominence also accrued to them. Because they served the high priest they thought that their word should determine the pace of things in the vestibule. Theirs was the sin of vanity, the vanity of the gossipy woman. Such vanity squelched the better urges of their hearts, smothered any sympathy they might have had for the friend of the prisoner, and enabled them to take delight in seeing the deadly fear which crept over Peter's features.

It is most likely that those maid-servants did not have the slightest notion of the significance of their sin. Later they probably had a good laugh together because of the embarrassment they had caused Peter. Doubtless, they complimented each other upon the clever manner in which they had disarmed him. By that self-satisfied laugh they suppressed the accusation of conscience. They smugly laughed while Peter wept bitterly in his deep remorse. But such laughing did not expiate their sin. They remained responsible for their conduct. All gossip and superficial prattle is sin. We are all familiar with the type. They are always giggling, and gossiping, and prattling. And always they take delight in embarrassing someone else. They never stop to think of the wounds they inflict, and never take note of the fact that the sin of superficial gossip frequently incriminates those who hear, even as it did Peter.

SUGGESTED QUESTIONS FOR STUDY AND DISCUSSION

1. Why was it peculiar to both of these maid-servants to provoke and ridicule Peter?

2. To what sin of Peter did this lead?

3. What is the teaching of this incident as to consideration for others, in every word and deed?

SAPPHIRA

But a certain man named Ananias, with Sapphira his wife, sold a possession, and kept back part of the price, his wife also being privy to it.

—Acts 5:1, 2.

READ: ACTS 5:1-11

GOD punished Sapphira by death because she acted falsely and dishonestly. Would you say that because of that she was so extraordinarily wicked that you would also be sure to throw her out of your Church as an outcast? This account in the Acts does not justify an affirmative answer to that question. She was a married woman, who lived on good terms with her husband, Ananias. It seems that they co-operated with each other in everything. Neither Sapphira nor her husband were worldly people, for they had definitely allied themselves with the Apostles. They had segregated themselves from Judaism and attached themselves to Jesus. No one can say that they merely professed to serve Christ. They were Christians in very deed, and did a thing which many highly reputed Christians never do: They sold a part of their property in order to present a gift to the Apostles, to be used either for the poor or for the public worship. These were very desirable activities which tend to put Sapphira in a favorable light.

Why, then, did God put her to death? Simply because she was dishonest in her relationship to God. A spirit had begun to permeate the Church at Jerusalem which induced men to feel loosely attached to property, and urged them to work in the direction of an equal distribution of it. That spirit, irrespective of the disastrous consequences to which it led, was sacred in its origin, for it illustrated that these Christians were not the servants of Mammon and that they loved the brethren. But the same thing occurred at Jerusalem which frequently occurs when essentially good movements are originated. These do not appeal equally to everyone, even though everyone wishes to seem to be co-operating with them. It is a situation like that which caused Ananias and Sapphira to sin.

They had not yet reached the point at which they cared to completely deny earthly possessions. They did not yet love the brethren enough to be willing to give them too much of their property. Who would have dared to call this attitude a sin? Did not Peter himself say: "While it remained, was it not thine own?" But these two people liked the affection and enthusiasm which the others displayed. People spoke praisingly of this person and of that, who had sold a piece of property for the common good. And it annoyed Ananias and Sapphira somewhat that they could not yet be included in that list of generous benefactors. In fact, if any comments were being made about them at all, they doubtless were intended to remind them of the fact that they, too, still had a piece of land to sell.

Hence, they began to consider the matter of selling their plot of ground. They refused to keep it any longer, it seemed to be constantly accusing them. They argued that as long as they still owned that property they would be regarded as unpious people by the Church. Therefore they concluded to sell it. They reached that conclusion not because they felt glad to sacrifice that property. By no means. They would have preferred to retain it. They did not determine to sell it because they loved their neighbor so very much. That love was not a particularly prominent characteristic in them. Their reason for selling their land was that they did not wish to be regarded as hoarders who thought only of themselves, now that so many others were selling their land. Hence, they mutually agreed to sell. Ananias said to his wife: "It's agreeable to you, isn't it? We'll sell the land."

The land was sold, and with it a great burden was lifted off their hearts. Before long, now, the people would also be saying that they, Ananias and Sapphira, had sold their property. Thus they did away with the rock of offense. And yet—dishonesty thus became a deliberate lie, no one would have to know how much they had received for the land. Accordingly the husband and the wife mutually agreed to keep a part of the money for themselves. Not so very much of course, not half of it for instance, because that would become too obvious. And they would have liked least of all to awaken suspicions. It should seem as if they had brought all of it to the Apostles.

If they had only been successful in that they would have been very happy. The entire congregation would be thinking of them as very pious people who had given their all for the Church. At the same time they could have hoarded a snug little sum in their cabinet at home.

Thus we see that they were not spiritually motivated. To make appearances resemble realities is dishonesty. And these two people meant to deceive themselves, the church, and, if possible, even God Himself. They were punished by death for that dishonesty. We do not know whether Peter had accidentally heard of the sale price of the land, or whether God revealed the deceit to him

It does not materially matter.   He knew that Sapphira
and her husband had deceived the Church of God.   Peter
became angry in the Lord's right.   He ripped the texture
which had been woven out of the threads of pious appearances and greediness to shreds.   As a warning to the
Church of the centuries, Ananias and Sapphira fell down
dead.   They did not enter into the peace of their God.

SUGGESTED QUESTIONS FOR STUDY AND DISCUSSION

1. What good deed did Ananias and Sapphira plan?
2. How did the devil frustrate their plans?
3. What was the condemnation of God on this deceit for
   temporal and eternal life?

MARY OF JERUSALEM

And when he had considered the thing, he came to the house of Mary the mother of John, whose surname was Mark; where many were gathered together praying.
—Acts 12:12.

READ: Acts 12:1-12

MARY of Jerusalem was a rich widow. We are assured of that fact by the circumstance that she owned a house which was large enough to accommodate the entire congregation. And, because we know that it had a gate, we have reason to believe that it belonged to the more conspicuous houses of Jerusalem. We know, besides, that she had a following of servants, of whom Rhoda, the maid-servant who had to open the door to Peter, is specifically named.

This Mary had joined the service of the Lord very early. She had become a Christian and enjoyed the happiness of observing that her son, Mark, became a minister of the Word. He accompanied Paul on one of his journeys, and to this day he speaks to the Church of God through his Gospel.

But we must limit our observations to the primary particulars which the Scriptures give us concerning her. They are these: She owned her own house, and gave it to the congregation for the purpose of worshipping God.

The congregation at Jerusalem did not just happen to be meeting at her house on this specific night. It was their custom to meet there regularly during the days of the persecution of Herod Agrippa. We may infer from the circumstance that Peter, the same moment in which

71

he was delivered from the prison, immediately determined to find the congregation at Mary's house. That
congregation did not yet possess a church building at
that time. They had at first met in one of the rooms of
the temple, but that had become impossible since Herod's
ire had been aroused. Then Mary had opened her house
to them. There the congregation of the Lord met to be
strengthened in the faith. There, too, they had met now
that they wished to pray for Peter.

Ask yourself for a moment, if you care to, how many
large houses with commodious rooms are standing vacant
in our cities, while Christian societies and organizations
experience the greatest possible difficulty in finding available meeting places. But who at present, like Mary,
would think of opening their own houses to the Christian
brothers and sisters, who would think of making one of
her rooms available to them? This is not a matter of
offering one's house for rent, but of giving it freely to
such services, simply because it pleases the owner to be
of service to God. Usually it is found that people then
think their houses too fashionable, their ornaments too
costly, and their furniture too beautiful to be subjected to
possible dishevelment. Many a Christian in our day
permits such rooms to remain vacant, and then pays a
few dollars to an organization with the firm belief that
he has been excessively liberal.

For that reason Mary's beautiful example appeals very
strongly, especially to widows whose husbands have died,
and whose children have already left their homes. Just
what do such widows do with those large houses, with
those uninhabited buildings, with those great hollow
rooms? Might not life be imparted to those dull corridors
if they were open to meetings for purposes of prayer and

for purposes of all kinds of Christian activity? How glorious it would be if the oppressive silence of such great rooms might be broken by the friendly music of an organ, accompanied by the voice of the singers of psalms.

We do not mean to say that this never happens. Thanks be God's for the fact that there are still brothers and sisters who convert their houses into open courts for the purposes of the people of God. The Marys of Jerusalem have not yet passed away. Nevertheless, they are too few in number. Too many organizations are still renting, in spite of the fact that many a house is standing vacant. Love still plays too small a role, and money too significant a part. This ought not to be so, for money freezes the hearts of men, while love melts them. To rent a room is to display no affection for a cause, but a free gift is in itself an edifying act.

Please do not reply that it costs too much trouble to receive people into your house, that it gets everything dirty, that it always must be cleaned and straightened out again. Surely, Mary, who was also a housewife, also knew all of these difficulties, and yet these were not sufficient to conquer her love for the Lord and for the brethren. Or perhaps you feel inclined to answer that for your own part you would be glad to do something like that, but that it causes all kinds of difficulties with the servant folk. In that case consider the character of Rhoda. She ran to open the door to Peter. Her voice betrayed nothing other than genuine and hearty joy as she did so. She seemed pleased to be able to co-operate with her mistress in the service of the Church of God. So far from causing your maid-servant any embarrassment, you will be likely to ingratiate yourself into her confidence. If that is not the result, you have the type of maid-servant who has no right to work in a Christian home.

SUGGESTED QUESTIONS FOR STUDY AND DISCUSSION

1. Which of the four Evangelists was the son of Mary?
2. In what specific way did she help the congregation of Christ at Jerusalem?
3. What particular message has this meditation for us?

RHODA

*And as Peter knocked at the door of the gate, a damsel
came to hearken, named Rhoda.*

—Acts 12:13.

Read: Acts 12:13-25

WE are not given very many particulars about Rhoda,
but the one trait in her character of which we are
told, enlightens us enough to justify us in giving her a
place in the traditions of Christianity. She is especially
significant because of her position as a maid-servant. She
served in the house of Mary the mother of Mark, who
lived in her own house at Jerusalem. The one incident
which is related concerning her is that she opened the door
to Peter, when he knocked at Mary's gate after his
miraculous escape from the prison.

On that occasion Rhoda appeared for a moment, and
then disappeared again. We hear no more of her. But
that one appearance reveals enough to us to give us an
insight into her position and character. Her appearance
in the Scriptures is especially significant because we are
told so very little about the kind of domestic life that was
lived in those first birthdays of the new life of Christianity.

There are three things about her which are worthy of
comment.

In the first place, she was a spiritual ally of the woman
she served. The small congregation gathered at Mary's
house to pray. Long after midnight the Christians of
Jerusalem were still gathered at her house to pray God

that Peter might be spared. As they all lay upon their knees in a prayerful attitude, Peter himself appeared at the gate and knocked for admittance. Rhoda was the first of those present to hear that knock. She proved throughout the incident that she was intensely interested in Peter's need and anxiety, and that she personally re joiced because of his freedom. We know that her response was such, for we read that when she heard Peter's voice, she ran to tell the others. When these heard her, they concluded that she was mad. Very obviously then, she worked for more than a mere salary. She confessed Mary's God, experienced the same spiritual life that Mary experienced, and shared in the joys and woes of the Church of God. Rhoda was, accordingly, an ideal maidservant, for nothing could praise her so much as the fact that she co-operated with her people in serving a larger purpose in the Church of God.

In addition to that great virtue, however, Rhoda embodied another. She served with readiness and dispatch. She was not one of those pious little weaklings who always let their work pile up, and who are completely unfit for their task. She stood at her post as a faithful servant should. Naturally, she would have greatly preferred to have been inside where the others were at prayer. In spite of that she remained out-of-doors because her duty demanded that she keep vigil over the house. Apparently Mary's house was separated from the street by a vestibule. Between the street and the vestibule there was a wall, and in that wall there was a gate. Rhoda took her position at that gate, while the others were praying inside of the house. She realized that no pious prayer could ever compensate for an unpious shirking of duty.

The third trait which appeals to us from Rhoda's character is her exuberant nature. She acted foolishly when she left Peter standing without as she went in to tell the others. Any woman characterized by a calmer, less passionate nature would have first unbolted the door, permitted Peter to enter, and would then have gone in to tell the congregation. But Rhoda was a spontaneous child of nature. She is chiefly concerned about Mary and the people of God. Now she saw that Peter was standing at the gate. She could think of nothing other than the impulse in her heart to tell those who were praying. The Scriptures tell us that in her gladness she ran within and interrupted the prayers by the announcement, "Peter standeth at the gate." Only when those within unanimously agreed that she was mad, did Rhoda run to produce the evidence. Then she first strode through the vestibule, unlocked the door, and let the apostle enter.

Suggested Questions for Study and Discussion

1. Does it appear as though Rhoda worked merely for her salary? Why?
2. How did she perform her duties? Was she a worker or a shirker?
3. What spirit seemed to permeate her work? What significance has it for us?

DORCAS, OR TABITHA

*Now there was at Joppa a certain disciple named Tabitha,
which by interpretation is called Dorcas: this woman was
full of good works and almsdeeds which she did.*

—Acts 9:36.

READ: ACTS 9:36-42

THE name of the wise and noble woman of Joppa
whom Peter raised from the dead was not Dorcas
but Tabitha. By birth she was not a woman of Greece,
but a Jewess. When Peter called her back to life, he
did not say, "Dorcas, arise!" but he said, "Tabitha,
arise!" But we are told in the account that Tabitha
when translated means Dorcas, which is the Greek word
for a hind or a fawn. It is, however, quite futile to try
to substitute her original name for the one given her by
translation. Dorcas is the name which has gained a
currency among the women's societies that have studied
her. In time Dorcas became the usual name for such
societies. "We're having 'Dorcas' tonight" simply means
that the sewing-club for the poor intends to meet. It is
a most appropriate name for that purpose, for she seems
to have been the first woman who was inspired by Christ
to be active in such works of love.

To be busy at sewing for the benefit of the poor is no
longer considered to be an unusual occupation. In fact,
this noble activity began to appeal so strongly that it
even became quite common in circles which could by no
means be characterized as Christian societies. But in the
old days this situation was quite different. Just think

of the poverty-stricken Lazarus. It will serve to point out that sympathy towards the poor was far less common in his age than it was in the time of King Solomon. And, among the pagans, the situation was even worse. Because of the mighty influence of the spirit of Christ the urge to care for the poor generously and whole-heartedly first came to expression in Jerusalem. There the care of the poor usually occurred through general appropriations. At Joppa, near by Jerusalem, such sympathy took the more touching form of personal responsibility, and in this way it included clothing as well as food. It was Tabitha who first sensed this special responsibility.

Tabitha counteracted to Jesus' words when He said: "I was naked, and ye did not clothe me." Accordingly, Jesus and not Tabitha was the origin of the movement of love which has since continued throughout nearly nineteen centuries and has supplied clothes for thousands of needy people. Your Jesus, Who radiated a Divine influence from His person and from His cross is also the one Who induced the human heart to engage in such work of mercy. He permitted Himself to be robbed of His own clothes and to be hanged nakedly upon the cross, not merely in order to replace it by the cloak of His righteousness, but also to clothe the needy and distressed.

For that reason Tabitha's being raised from the dead has a special significance. By completing that miraculous wonder the Lord placed His Divine stamp of approval upon the work of caring for the poor which Tabitha introduced. She lived in order that she might devote her life to his genuinely Christian philanthropy. She made all her means available for that purpose. She did more than merely donate a gift now and then. Instead, she devoted all of her energy to the work. We read that she "was full of good works and almsdeeds which she did."

Because she was an indispensable boon in her community, her death caused a great deal of excitement in the beautiful haven. In such port-cities of that day, when sailing demanded many human sacrifices, there were always many women who had been left widows by the death of their husbands at sea. It was for these women that Tabitha had felt a special compassion.

It soon became apparent that these works of mercy were being followed by spiritual results. Love caused a return of love. Tabitha had loved those widows, and in return for her love these widows loved Tabitha. These women wept not merely because the loss would affect them concretely, but also because they loved Tabitha. When Peter came to Joppa he found them standing around her body with tears in their eyes. In this instance the jealousy, hatred, and greediness which always tends to separate one class of society from another had become completely obliterated. The power of eternal life entered the little city, and that Divine power alleviated human distress. It blessed the alms that had been given and bound rich and poor together by the bonds of an inner attachment.

For that reason Tabitha's name goes much farther than the aforementioned Dorcas societies. Tabitha gave expression to the principle out of which all Christian philanthropy must arise. That principle presents a beautiful calling to the woman who has no specific vocation in life. It teaches us that the curse of poverty can be removed only in the name of Jesus.

Suggested Questions for Study and Discussion

1. Why is it that women's societies frequently take the name of Dorcas?
2. How would you characterize Dorcas?
3. Does Dorcas appear to have had "saving faith"? Does this characterize the Dorcas Society of today?

MARY OF ROME

Greet Mary, who bestowed much labor on us.
—Rom. 16:6.

A T the close of his letter to the Church at Rome Paul sends his Apostolic greetings to not less than twenty individuals, each of whom he designates by name. Among these was a certain Roman woman who very likely had adopted the name of Mary at the time of her baptism. For Paul says of her, "Greet Mary, who bestowed much labor upon us." This Mary shared the honor of being mentioned so significantly with another Roman woman, whose name was Persis. Concerning her, Paul wrote, "Salute the beloved Persis, which laboured much in the Lord."

Later theologians inferred from these statements that Mary and Persis were evangelists, who were employed to engage in making propaganda in the same way in which the Salvation Army now employs women for that purpose. However, there is nothing to warrant such an inference. Romans sixteen tells us nothing about it. At the same time, however, our marginal commentators have under-estimated the value of the activities of these two women. These state that Mary merely extended her hospitality to those who brought the Gospel, that she merely proffered domestic services in the way that Mary of Bethany had done.

The fact that Paul says of Persis that she labored "in the Lord" gives us reason to believe that these women did more than that. It is true that she was not a deaconess, for had that been the case, the matter would have been differently expressed. Nor was she a public speaker, for, so far from praising her for that, Paul would have expressed his disapproval. But it may safely be inferred that she was a woman who exerted her influence in every possible way to advance the Lord's cause.

The fact that we can not give such activity a specific name by no means implies that the scope of its influence is limited. A woman of some standing can, if she proceeds tactfully, command many occasions in which to unobtrusively foster or hinder a cause. She can exert an influence upon her husband, and upon his associates, upon her children and upon the families of their playmates. Either she allies herself with or she opposes Christian tendencies among her friends and neighbors.

But, irrespective of that unconsciously leavening influence, such a woman can prove a boon to the Lord's cause by more direct means. In the days of the Church of Rome there were converted women who lived unhappily because they were married to pagan husbands. Converted maid-servants had been compelled to serve in pagan homes. There were children who desired baptism, but who were prevented from receiving it by their parents. Prisoners were submitted to severe trials for the Gospel's sake. Blasphemous rumors were circulated. Many homes forbade the entrance of those who would bring the Gospel. And in each of these circumstances women such as Mary and Persis could achieve great things for the Church of God. We sense that most clearly, perhaps, when we stop to think of the harm women can accomplish, even in the homes of preachers, when they are enemies of the faith. In that way we believe, then, that Mary of Rome abetted the Lord's cause, in that manner "she laboured much in the Lord." We are pleased to believe, besides, of course, that she proffered hospitality unstintedly, and that she aided the church by assisting in the collection of money.

For that reason, we may not fail to appreciate Mary's type of service. She was very different from Mary of Bethany, from Mary the mother of the apostle, and from Mary of Jerusalem. She revealed a capacity peculiar to herself, a capacity which should still be exercised in the congregation of God.

A woman who really loves Jesus must place all she has upon His altar, and that includes the influence which her social position gives her. Those who do not love Him do all they can to hinder His Church. Therefore Jesus may expect that those who love Him exert their energies strenuously to help His sacred cause to prosper. In this matter, too, talents are too frequently buried; gifts are allowed to lie fallow, and energies to remain latent.

This does not imply that a woman must forsake her home. Neither does it suggest that she must forsake all contact with the world. It means that she ought to plan how best she can influence old and young in her community, that she ought to exert herself to praise her Lord.

Mary was not an intriguing woman. But a woman frequently proves to be amazingly ingenious and energetic in the care of her husband and children. She should give full expression to that same ingenuity and energy in her endeavors for the Lord.

SUGGESTED QUESTIONS FOR STUDY AND DISCUSSION

1. Were Mary and Persis evangelists?
2. What did these women do on which Paul commented?
3. What can we learn from Mary's type of service?
4. Who are the six Marys mentioned in the New Testament?

LOIS

*When I call to remembrance the unfeigned faith that is
in thee, which dwelt first in thy grandmother Lois, and
thy mother Eunice; and I am persuaded that in thee also.*
—II TIM. 1:5.

READ: II TIM. 1

Lois is the "grandmother" of the Scriptures. In her is
revealed the peculiar significance of the grandmother
in a family. She represents, among the women of the
Bible, the spiritual influence which can issue from her
peculiar position.

Lois had been a believing woman. It seems obvious
that she had already died at the time that Paul sent his
second letter to Timothy. But he confirmed in that
letter that she had lived in unfeigned faith. Irrespective,
however, of when she had died, we can observe the important fact that the influence of her life had not been
buried with her. Observe, that the Holy Apostle
definitely relates the faith which was revealed in Timothy
to that which his mother Eunice had embodied, and
which, in turn, had been dominant in Lois before her.
These three links are nicely joined together, and, accordingly, form a spiritual chain. And behind the inter-
relation of these three revelations of faith there lies a
blood relationship. Physically, too, Timothy had been
born of Eunice and Eunice of Lois. In these generations,
therefore, the spiritual life kept pace and ran parallel
with the physical life. To the ties of blood were added
those of faith. Those ties of blood always pass from
child to child, and in this case the bonds of faith similarly

passed from one soul to that of the next generation. Lois did not, of course, give Eunice her faith, nor did Eunice impart hers to Timothy. God alone is the Author of faith. But the faith which God imparts must blossom into an active faith. And Lois fostered that graduation in Eunice, even as Eunice, by her fervor, in turn, fostered it in Timothy.

This happy relationship was the result of the Covenant of grace. God could have caused His elect to have been born in another home and in a different family. However, He usually does not do that. Sometimes, it is true, Christians arise from pagan homes. But that is not the general rule. As a rule the elect are born from families in which a mother or a grandmother has previously chosen for the Lord.

In this way, first internally, and then externally, the Lord envelops His chosen ones in Covenant grace. That grace is reflected in baptism, and permeates Christian training. It tends to make Christian family traditions binding. Hence, we treasure Paul's remembrance of Eunice and Lois. It seems to weave a holy bond around the generations, around parents, and children and grandchildren.

Sometimes the holy election leaps over a generation, grandmother and grandchild are saved, but the mother remains unconverted. In such instances the responsibility of the grandmother to her grandchild is exceptionally exacting. God then enables her to give her granddaughter what He withheld her own child from receiving. And in this way the stream of grace flows on uninterruptedly. But the grandmother's duty remains equally beautiful in those cases in which the mother also knows the Lord. Her responsibility still obtains when the children have married and have left the home. The mother is busy, and often quite fatigued by her faith. Grandmother lives a quieter life; her face reveals greater calm and greater peace. And when her grandchild receives the admonishings of faith from her lips, they seem to be stamped with the affirmation of many generations.

In this way the grandmother can impart what the mother, because of her briefer experience and busier life, can not yet give. She ought not to thwart the ardor of youth, ought not to take the mother's place, and regard the children as her own. She must give both mother and children that higher, unique blessing, which an aged woman with a rich spiritual experience alone can give.

SUGGESTED QUESTIONS FOR STUDY AND DISCUSSION

1. Did the influence of Lois' life bring Timothy to salvation?
2. Did Eunice impart her faith to Timothy?
3. What lesson may we learn from the relationship between Lois, Eunice and Timothy?

EUNICE

When I call to remembrance the unfeigned faith that is in thee, which dwelt first in thy grandmother Lois, and thy mother Eunice; and I am persuaded that in thee also.
—II TIM. 1:5.

READ: II TIM. 1

HOLY practices and pious traditions prevailed in the family out of which the Lord gave Timothy to the Church. We know three generations of them. First there is Timothy, behind him stood Eunice, and behind her, Lois. Through the veins of these three generations there coursed "unfeigned faith." The apostle confirms that such was the faith which was expressed first in Lois, then in Eunice and, finally, in Timothy.

In this way faith passed from child to grandchild. The mothers, of course, did not impart that faith to their children, for faith is and will ever remain the gift of God. It pleased Him to permit the blessings of the Covenant of grace to accrue to three generations. Thus God impressed upon them the value of what is abiding and lasting, and the consciousness that they were called as a family to glorify the name of the Lord.

Naturally, Lois did not know beforehand that her grandchild should occupy so prominent a place in the Church of Christ. Nor could Eunice have surmised that. But Paul does specifically call Timothy's attention to the fact that his faith is related to that of his mother and grandmother by intimate, spiritual bonds.

Such faith, like a kind of spiritual nobility, strongly attracts Paul, for he says that he desires greatly to see him, that he may be filled with joy at witnessing this sacred family. For Paul as an Israelite, a newly accomplished faith has even less appeal than this historically rooted belief. He thinks it strikingly beautiful that three successive generations should enter heaven. He revels in the contemplation of it.

But Paul tells us more than that. Eunice, Timothy's mother, is not mentioned merely to complete the cycle, to supply a missing link. Paul wishes to call our attention to what she accomplished as a mother, to the manner in which God used her and Lois as a means to inspire a palpitatingly real and fervent faith in Timothy.

"That you have always been schooled in the Scriptures," Paul tells Timothy in effect, "represents an invaluable grace, for which you ought always to thank your God." True, like a piece of firewood, one can be snatched from the flames late in life. Examples can be named of men and women, who were converted at advanced ages and who, nevertheless, were led far into the knowledge of God. But these are exceptions. It is better and safer for the child to be trained in the meaning of the Scriptures. The young human heart and spirit and conscience is far more susceptible to profound and lasting impressions than is the aged person. The child is very impressionable, has a vivid imagination and a concentration which assists memory. The child is docile and pliable and possesses that wholesome naivete which makes him eager to live vicariously in the world of the Scriptures. It had been Timothy's privilege to be trained in this way. To him the knowledge of the Scriptures and the content of faith were vividly real. They had not been made tempting to him by much polishing and furbishing, nor had they been superimposed upon him. Hence, they had not become superficial, but had grown into maturity together with his life and consciousness, and had thus become his true possession.

Timothy owed that invaluable training to his mother Eunice, even as Augustine owed his to Monica. That is not every son's privilege, for there are mothers, even among Christians, who shirk their high responsibility in this respect. In fact, there are children of God who later affirm that they never received a single spiritual blessing from their mother. But, at other times, God directs matters differently and inspires maternal hearts to plan and execute a holy activity. Many years later a converted son recalls that activity as the dearest and holiest of his memories of her. Something rich and glorious permeates such spiritual bands. The tenderness of maternal love is then sanctified by the love of Christ, and the urge to win her child for the Saviour is made fervent by the glowing ardor of her maternal heart. A mother such as that does not rest satisfied with permitting her son to read parables and stories from the Bible, but induces him to marvel at the rich and complete figure of his or her Saviour as He is there revealed.

We frequently lament the fact that mature sons fall from faith. But is there not also some room for lamentations when we feel compelled to ask where the Eunices are, where those intensely spiritual mothers are, who, because of their own ardent love for Christ, permit some of that love to flow into the hearts of their children? True, the fathers also have a blessed responsibility, and there are occasions on which the stronger character of the husband must guide the children in the home. But the husband can hardly be successful in his efforts, when these are not preceded by the tender spiritual activity of a pious, faithful, and praying mother. Mothers must begin that activity when their children are still very, very young. No, their object should not merely be to teach their children poise and manners. It does not suffice to prepare their food and to make their little beds inviting. What is far more necessary is that they lead their children into the mysteries of God.

SUGGESTED QUESTIONS FOR STUDY AND DISCUSSION

1. Does Paul value the home training of Timothy?
2. Are we still emphasizing the need for children being trained in the home?
3. What lesson has the life of Eunice for mothers of today?

JEZEBEL

Notwithstanding, I have a few things against thee, because thou sufferest that woman Jezebel, which calleth herself a prophetess, to teach and to seduce my servants to commit fornication, and to eat things sacrificed unto idols.
—REV. 2:20.

READ: REV. 2:20-24

THE detrimental influences of a sibyl became evident in the church at Thyatira very soon after its inception. The Scriptures tell us that she was called Jezebel, but they do not indicate whether that was actually her name, or whether, because of her practices, she was called a second Jezebel as a happily characterizing nickname.

It was discovered not long ago from other sources, that at that time such a sibyl had indeed appeared in Thyatira. It was learned that an exceptionally influential woman had arisen in that city during the second half of the first century, that she had established her headquarters in a beautiful temple just outside of the town, and that she had become very popular because of her fortune-telling. And it is easily understood that many of her group should early have felt inclined to affiliate themselves with the Church of Christ. Such sibyls had the habit of sketching the coming of a Utopia to the masses, as well as the coming of terrible events and of a right-about-face alteration in religious affairs.

The first messengers of Christ to appear in Thyatira seemed to be preaching the coming of very similar events. To all appearances, they preached a new religion, the end of the world, and the return of Christ.

This message seemed to cohere beautifully with what the sibyl had told them, and hence it is not surprising that many recognized in it the fulfilment of Jezebel's words, and that they accordingly hastened to join the Church. Naturally their affiliation was not the result of grace. It rested entirely upon the false basis of fictive fortune-telling. Their identification with the Church of Christ by no means implied, therefore, that they had forsaken the sibyl, that they had turned their backs to Jezebel. In fact, it meant that they thought even more highly of her than they had done before. "Observe!" they said to each other, "Her predictions become fulfilled!"

In this way there arose among that group a sinful mixture of Christian confessions with idolatrous necromancy. This situation resulted in the pathetic circumstance that the sinful view of life which Jezebel augmented began to dominate over that spiritual integrity which Christianity preached. And these people induced many weaker Christians to also surrender to the false tendency. Hence, there arose in the Church at Thyatira a most undesirable situation. Spiritually those who were led astray adhered to a most sentimental fanaticism. Besides, they indulged in terrible wantonness and positive fornication. For that reason Jesus warned in His letter to the church at Thyatira: "I hold it against thee that thou permittest the woman Jezebel, who poses as a prophetess to teach and to seduce my servants to commit fornication, and to eat things sacrificed unto idols." Later Christ Himself afflicted this woman with a terrible disease. "Behold," he says in the letter, "I will cast her into a bed, I will kill her children with death; and all the churches shall know that I am he which searches the reins and hearts." In this way that great evil was thwarted, not of its own accord, but by a mighty intervention of the Lord. By His providential counsel He Himself purged the Church at Thyatira.

But the fact remains, nevertheless, that that newly organized Church of the Lord became guilty of most unscrupulous conduct when, in an uprush of spiritual fanaticism, it embraced the demoniacal spirit of pagan necromancy. Instead of glorifying her God, that Church profaned the name of the Lord.

The imminent danger which lurked beneath the deceit of this sibyl has, therefore, been included in the Scriptures, in order to demonstrate to the church of successive ages what the inevitable consequences are when these abandon the simplicity of the faith, pursue whatever happens to pique the curiosity, and interweave all kinds of worldly guesses with the preaching of the Gospel. The holy simplicity of the Gospel does not satisfy curiosity-mongers. Whoever tries to make it do so will find that the Church of Christ soon becomes an artificial formalism which serves to assure all types of ungodly spirits an influential position.

Such decadence becomes doubly dangerous whenever a woman has a hand in the matter. A woman ought not to presume to teach in the Church of Christ or to desire to be a leader of spirits there. But if she insists upon doing so, and if she then borrows her effectiveness from the strange and occult, then the Church incurs the danger of incongruously intermingling flesh and spirit. The Scriptures have given us a poignant picture of such incongruity in revealing the abhorrent conduct of the Nicolaitans. For these were not men and women who conducted themselves piously and chastely in public in order to indulge fornication in secret. They were people who set up a diabolically inspired rationalization which suggested that such indulgence was an earmark of intensely spiritual living.

These all are spiritual atrocities which have manifested themselves repeatedly in the Church throughout the centuries. And, in the form of Anti-Nomianism, they periodically reappear in our own age and country. We ought constantly to inspire a righteous indignation against these manifestations. Never for the space of a moment lend an ear to the sinful conversations of such people. They argue it so convincingly, do they? What of that? Your own conviction, certainly, assures you that Christ can have no communion with this Belial. Remember, however, to distinguish between those who tempt and those who are tempted. Whoever fosters such decadence must with righteous indignation be punished and be excommunicated from the church. But those who have been led astray, those who have been lured and ensnared by this tempting but poisonous bait, must be admonished. Induce their consciences to accuse them, and draw them back by your faithful love. For these must be saved

SUGGESTED QUESTIONS FOR STUDY AND DISCUSSION

1. Why was Jezebel a hindrance to the Church of Thyatira?

2. What curse did Christ pronounce upon her?

3. Are we in danger, today, of being led astray by women like Jezebel?

LYDIA

And a certain woman named Lydia, a seller of purple, of the city of Thyatira, which worshipped God, heard us: whose heart the Lord opened, that she attended unto the things which were spoken of Paul.

—Acts 16:14.

READ: ACTS 16:14-40

L YDIA had lived at Thyatira, the same city in which the sibyl Jezebel tried to lead God's people astray. At the time she met Paul, however, she lived at Philippi.

She kept a shop from which she sold dyed garments, for we are told that she was a seller of purple. This does not mean to suggest that she merely sold purple. Our druggists do not sell drugs merely, but soaps and lotions and many articles besides. In this same sense, Lydia, although she was called a seller of purple, doubtless traded in many articles besides. Her home must have been amply spacious, for she was in a position to accommodate Paul and Silas and whoever else accompanied him, there.

We do not know whether or not she was of Jewish descent. At all events, she had become converted to the God of Israel, for we observe that on the Sabbath day she joined other Jewish women at the accustomed meeting place. That place was not the Synagogue, for that institution, obviously, did not yet then exist at Philippi. In such localities the Jews had formed the custom of meeting outside of the city in some meadow or shaded place. There they did not observe the usual form of service, but merely gathered in common prayer. At Philippi a shaded open plain upon the river's banks served for that purpose. That river is at present called the Maritza. Because of the islet which divides it into two streams, it still lends that prominent city an inviting appearance. Upon visiting it, the place where the Jews joined in common prayer is still pointed out to one. It is unwise, of course, to place unequivocal confidence in such a tradition as that which names these facts. But it is possible, nevertheless, to vividly picture the atmosphere of those gatherings to ourselves. How those Jewish women seated themselves upon the banks of that river. How Paul and Silas went there to announce to them that the Messiah whom they awaited had appeared in Jesus of Nazareth.

It seems, however that Paul did not find many attentive hearts among those women. For Lydia's acceptance of his words is reported as if it was an exception, and that circumstance suggests that most of the others rejected it.

Apparently, Paul had just arrived at Philippi, had been there only a few days, and during that time had found no opportunity to meet with the people and to find an audience for his message. For that reason he awaited the Sabbath. Naturally, Lydia also on that day closed up the shop. Led by her God, she went to the place of prayer.

Paul's preaching could not effect her regeneration. The external call never accomplishes that, unless the internal call to repentance precedes, and unless it accompanies the Word. Concerning Lydia's conversion we read specifically that "the Lord opened her heart." Why hers and not those of the other women? Who can answer that? The Lord is sovereign. He chooses, and by free grace. And it is now as it was then. The missionary who goes out can bring no one to life, if God has not His elect among the heathen, be they Turks or Jews. Except the Lord's grace precede, the work of the missionary is futile and purposeless.

Lydia was an elect of the Lord. He had penetrated her heart with conquering grace. He had converted her. Hence that man Paul fascinated her. She assimilated what she heard. She actually understood, while the others merely heard syllables pronounced or, perhaps, laughed at his words. A flame was lighted in her soul. She reached out her hand to the Christ Paul preached. Yes, she believed.

Then her heart urged her to hear more, and also to offer her assistance to these servants of the Lord. They had to "put up" in a mean hotel. As the situation was in those days, that circumstance could only injure their purpose. For such inns were at that time tryingly inconvenient and were almost exclusively patronized by the baser class of people. Lydia, accordingly, at once insisted that Paul and Silas stay at her home. Apparently, she was an unmarried woman, a widow, perhaps. But she was a shopkeeper and used to public contacts. That experience helped her master her reticence, and she accordingly invited the men to her home.

She did not offer them this convenience as a service, but begged for it as a favor. "If ye have judged me to be faithful to the Lord," she said, "come into my house and abide there." True, Paul hesitated for a moment. But she insisted, and Paul yielded. Literally, we read, "and she constrained us."

It appears that those who lived at her house with her shared Lydia's faith that the Messiah should come, for these also confessed the Christ and were baptized with her.

In this way she accommodated Paul and Silas for a few days. They stayed at her home until the riot arose in which they were made prisoners. It must have been an anxious day for Lydia when Paul did not return, and when it was reported to her that he and Silas were in chains. You may safely suppose that she and her housemates spent hours in prayer and supplication for Paul. And it seems that the other converts at Philippi joined with her in prayer at her home. In this way they anxiously bided time until they heard a knock at the door, and until Paul and Silas, miraculously delivered by God from the cell, again stood before them.

We read that then Paul and Silas again entered the house and for the last time enjoyed Lydia's generous hospitality. They returned thanks to God. Paul warned the brethren that terrible trials also hung suspended over their heads. Then he parted from this pious woman, in whom God had glorified His grace; and who, because of what she did for Paul, continues after eighteen centuries to be a sacred memory to the people of God.

SUGGESTED QUESTIONS FOR STUDY AND DISCUSSION

1. Where did Lydia live? What was her occupation?
2. How and where were the services conducted which Lydia attended?
3. What does the life of Lydia teach?

PRISCILLA

Greet Priscilla and Aquila, my helpers in Christ Jesus.
—Rom. 16:3.

Read: Acts 18:2, 3, 26; Rom. 16:3; I Cor. 16:19;
II Tim. 4:19

Prisca (II Tim. 4:19) or Priscilla (Rom. 16:3) was a
Jewish woman who belonged to the better middle class.
Her husband, Aquila, kept a canvas-maker's shop, the
chief business of which consisted of making canvases for
tents. This husband and wife had originally come from
Pontus, but because they were enterprising business
people, they had decided against this quiet town in favor
of Rome, the seat of the empire, as their home. There
they succeeded in business until Claudius, by exiling all
the Jews, also drove this couple out of that cosmopolitan
city. They then went by boat to Corinth, one of the
ranking commercial cities of that day. There they met
the holy apostle, Paul.

One is inclined to believe that they were still typical
Jews at this time, and that Paul offered them his services
as an assistant at the making of tents. Had he been a
Christian at that time, one can hardly understand how
Aquila could have countenanced seeing this single apostle
of the Lord expend his precious time at sewing canvases.
One would say that this could not have been made possible. Paul was but a single man. To have "boarded"
him could have presented no insurmountable difficulties.
Indeed, it seems that if they had been believers they
could have done nothing else, now that this apostle of

the Lord was with them, than to have considered it a privilege to have welcomed this ambassador of God into their family circle. Of course, it might have altered matters some, if the man had had an unwilling wife. But God had granted Aquila a most energetic and wise help-meet in Priscilla. At Ephesus they opened their house to the Church for purposes of worship (I Corinthians 16:19). Their house, therefore, must have been com-modious enough to entertain an entire congregation. How could they, then, have permitted Paul to sew tent covers, if they already then acknowledged that he was an apostle of Christ?

Accordingly, it is more plausible to think of the matter in this way. Paul, who had previously learned the trade, had presented himself to them when they were still Jews. In this way he was given occasion to make contact with the family, and thus the Gospel of Christ entered the home. Hence, too, it goes without saying that Priscilla, after her conversion, soon put a stop to Paul's work at the shop, and assigned to him an honorable place in her home. She must have removed from before him every obstacle which hindered his glorifying Christ as King in the streets of Corinth. She who in a crucial moment had risked her life for Paul, could impossibly have with-held from him the necessaries of life.

For we may remember that Priscilla was by no means a superficial convert. She was not a "goody-goody" per-son, quite surfeited with unctious sentiment, one who regarded the truth of secondary importance. We find many such confessors of the Christ among the higher and lower strata of society, women who seem to be inter-ested, who are touched by spiritual urges, but who never think of profoundly penetrating the truth. But Priscilla was far too substantial to be satisfied with emotional superficiality, and just because of that Paul appealed so strongly to her. For, in her home Paul was not only a teacher of the Christ but also a family friend and an intellectual companion. And we have every reason to believe that Paul, too, found his setting gratifyingly congenial.

Obviously, Priscilla was a woman who had been thoroughly schooled in the Scriptures as a Jewess. She listened with concentrated attention to what the Lord's apostle revealed, grasped the import of the profound concepts of God's Kingdom, was personally moved by them, understood them, and at the end was almost in a position to teach others the truth of God. We know that from the incidents involving Apollos at Ephesus.

Apollos was a prominent man and a ready orator. He had become somewhat acquainted with the Christ by means of the disciples of John, but he had never appreciated the pith and core of the Christian Religion. In spite of that, however, he on one occasion spoke to the congregation while it met in Priscilla's house in Ephesus. Priscilla heard him. And when she observed how hopelessly confused the kindly-intending Apollos was, she, so far from publicly disparaging him, called him apart "and expounded unto him the way of God more perfectly." By "more perfectly" is meant that she expounded the way of God more painstakingly, more precisely, and more accurately. Apollos had heard a thing or two but had by no means comprehended the significance of it all. His conceptions were vague and his presentation abounded in platitudes and in grand, meaningless words. Priscilla detected at once that such preaching carried no weight and opened the way for numerous heresies besides. Then this remarkable woman, inasmuch as no teacher was present, took upon herself the duty of exposing the Christian Religion to Apollos, and caused him to comprehend clearly the weighty significance of the plan of salvation.

A woman such as Priscilla was, is a potent influence in any congregation to which she happens to belong, and we might wish that we could point out ten or twenty such women in each of our larger congregations. From her position in the Word of God she affirms that a woman, also a married woman, has another calling besides those of dispatching daily duties and engaging in activities of mercy. A woman, too, must have faith, and that faith must borrow its strength from a knowledge of the truth.

How many young married men might have been saved if their mothers had been Priscillas to them? In that lies the strength of a Priscilla. She knows the truth, and knows how to present it with perfect clarity. Besides, she has the ingratiating tenderness of feminine appeal, a quality no man has.

Priscilla later returned to Rome. Tradition has it that she died as a martyr for the name of the Lord. Perhaps this report is unfounded. This, however, is certain: she was a witness for the Lord. After her conversion her whole life represented self-sacrifice and a consecration of all her capacities to the cause of Christ.

SUGGESTED QUESTIONS FOR STUDY AND DISCUSSION

1. How did Aquila and Priscilla make the acquaintance of Paul?
2. Was Priscilla well grounded in the faith?
3. Is caring for the household the only responsibility of women? What does the life of Priscilla teach concerning this?

DRUSILLA

And after certain days, when Felix came with his wife Drusilla, which was a Jewess, he sent for Paul, and heard him concerning the faith in Christ.

—ACTS 24:24.

READ: ACTS 24:25-27

DRUSILLA came from Edom. She was the daughter of the Idumaean king, Herod Agrippa, and was born in the year 34 A.D. Just as did her people, so Drusilla professed the Jewish religion. To her as to them the call of the Lord came through the mouth of Paul. She was asked to kneel before Zion's Anointed King.

At the time when she heard Paul at Caesarea she had not yet reached the age of twenty, but in spite of her youth she had already passed an eventful life. She was a young woman of rare beauty, and that beauty had been the cause of terrible moral decadence in her. As a girl of fifteen or sixteen years she had married Prince Azizus, the king of Emesa. But instead of remaining faithful to him she had left him and had illegitimately married the Roman governor, Felix. That had happened in this way. Felix had met her at court festivities, and was so enamored of her Oriental beauty that he at once planned to abduct her. Surely he, the governor of mighty Rome, has as little to fear from impotent King Azizus as the Netherlands' governor at Java from the prince of Djokjo. And Drusilla, who felt flattered by the thought that this mighty governor was paying her attentions, by no means repelled his advances. It is true that she did not immediately consent. But Felix sent Simon, a Jewish necromancer, to her, and after a little resistance, she succumbed to the wishes of this clever artificer, quietly left the court of Azizus, and soon afterwards married Felix. Her marriage, accordingly, was doubly sinful: she married a heathen who did not confess the faith of her fathers; and she married him illegally inasmuch as her first husband was still living when she yielded to Felix. Azizus, naturally, could do nothing about it. In this instance, too, sheer might concealed the guilt. And Drusilla was not ashamed to appear in public as the wife of Felix.

She had been married to the heathen governor approximately a year when Paul came to Caesarea as a prisoner. It seems that this event piqued her curiosity. When Felix had Paul appear before him, she was an auditor. Rumors concerning the Christ had also reached her ears. Naturally, Drusilla also wanted to see a representative of the sect, and to hear what kind of tale he told. Well, she heard it. Standing eloquently before her, the apostle and witness of the Lord announced to her also, that the Star of Jacob had arisen, and that the Lord had visited His people. And Paul did more than that. Naturally, he knew much better than we do all the details of Drusilla's sinful life, and it must have grieved him to observe that a young Jewish woman had thus deserted the faith of her fathers. And it vexed him still more, doubtless, to acknowledge that this young girl by leaving Azizus and marrying Felix had cruelly and unscrupulously trodden God's commandment under foot.

Because of this terrible offense, Paul, in fulfilling his duty, overlooked and diminished nothing, but passionately directed a message of righteousness, temperance, and judgment to Felix and his Drusilla. He spoke to them of righteousness, for her treatment of Azizus had represented a breach of law and of faith. He spoke of temperance, for her desire for power and luxury had induced her to illegitimately marry Felix. And he spoke of judgment. Did everything seem to be going smoothly now? No matter, that. God's judgment would certainly accrue to such sinful conduct.

That judgment came, in time. It was less severe for Felix. He was the lesser responsible of the two. As a heathen he knew no better. And Paul's preaching affected him, it provoked fear in his heart.

But the full force of the judgment came upon Drusilla. She, too, felt the arrow which Paul shot into her conscience. But she proudly resisted its pain, she kicked against the goads, and laughed at the man's entertaining earnestness. Twenty years later the awful eruption of Vesuvius occurred, by which flourishing Pompeii and Herculaneum were buried under burning lava. Many fled at that time, and by fleeing, many escaped the catastrophe. But Drusilla, who just at that moment was bringing her only child, Agrippa, to Pompeii, did not escape. Either she was warned too late, or she underestimated the danger. Josephus tells us that she and her child were also buried beneath the lava.

She had laughed at "right," had mocked temperance. In that moment the judgment came.

Drusilla, who had dishonored her faith, rejected the preaching of Christ, forsaken her husband, and lived on in sinful wedlock—that Drusilla learned how awful it is to fall into the hands of a living God.

SUGGESTED QUESTIONS FOR STUDY AND DISCUSSION

1. How is the early life of Drusilla a warning to young women of today?
2. Where did Drusilla first meet Paul?
3. Did Drusilla suffer for her early sin? If so, in what way?

EUODIAS AND SYNTYCHE

I beseech Euodias, and beseech Syntyche, that they be of the same mind in the Lord.

—PHIL. 4:2.

READ: PHIL. 4

WOMEN have assumed a large role in the introduction of Christianity in the world of heathendom. From the greetings included in the close of Paul's letters we glean the names of a large number of these influential women. In Rome alone there were Phebe of Cenchrea, Mary, "who bestowed much labour upon us," Tryphena and Tryphosa, "who labour in the Lord," Persis, "which laboured much in the Lord," and, in addition, Julia, a sister of Nereus. Certainly, this constitutes a rich register of names, and all of them were women upon whose assistance in the Gospel Paul strongly relied. At Philippi the same circumstance was true. At first Lydia, the seller of purple, occupied the foreground. And now we read of two other influential women, named Euodias and Syntyche, concerning whom Paul boasts that they were women "which laboured with me in the Gospel, with Clement also, and with other of my fellow-labourers."

Both of them must therefore have been women who, at Paul's arrival at Philippi, belonged to the first who accepted the Gospel. And they belonged to those, too, who immediately offered Paul their services, and whose active, feminine assistance helped to make the Church at Philippi manifest. Nor was their activity the momentary flare of temporary enthusiasm. On the con-

108

trary, they remained active after the Church had been definitely established. At the time when Clement, first, and others later, came to head this flourishing congregation, these women were still persevering in their holy endeavor and were consecrating their talents to the growth of the Church.

But, alas! Dissension arose between Euodias and Syntyche, and this, naturally, worked havoc for the church. The enemy rejoiced, but the congregation grieved. Paul does not tell us about what they differed. Whether one of them became jealous of the other, whether the one wished to go about the work differently from the other, whether Euodias traversed Syntyche's domains, or whether Syntyche seemed more successful, we do not know. No one can ever determine that. At any rate Cain and Abel repeated themselves. As a result the congregational work lagged, and the progress of the Gospel was retarded.

What did Paul do about it? Shrug his shoulders dubiously, perhaps, and, although he found it painful, permit the quarrel to quietly continue? By no means. Such dissension may not be left undisturbed in a congregation. That would be dishonoring the Lord's name. It would induce men to mock the church. It would have hindered the progress of grace in Euodias and Syntyche. When such quarrels arise between influential persons, factions of the congregation generally rally to the side of one or the other. If that had happened at Philippi, God's grace and blessing would have departed from that congregation.

Hence, Paul wrote: Stop that quarrel between Euodias and Syntyche. Have no patience with it. Because they have been purchased and are owned by one Lord, they must be of the same mind in Christ.

And we ought to remember, too, that without referring to these women by name, he also stated in that letter: "If there be therefore any consolation in Christ, if any comfort of love, if any fellowship of the spirit, if any bowels and mercies, fulfil ye my joy, that ye be like-minded, having the same love, being of one accord, of one mind. Let nothing be done through strife or vain-glory; but in lowliness of mind let each esteem other better than themselves." Judge for yourself, whether in writing these words Paul was not thinking first of all of Euodias and Syntyche.

Paul goes farther than that, however. He knows that he has a friend at Philippi, a certain Syzygos, who can influence these women. Paul advises this man as to his duty in the matter, by urging him to quench the fires of contention. Paul writes that Syzygos is to "help those women." That was the appropriate advice to give. Christians who are divided by quarrels and dissensions must be "helped." Both parties want peace. Each asks God to restore it. But they can not help themselves. Hence, the love of the other brothers and sisters must come to their assistance.

That is the course events took at Philippi. There is no doubt about it. The fires of dissension died because they were immediately quenched. Quick action was necessary. When such conflagrations first begin one can extinguish them with his feet. But if these are permitted to burn on, the entire church can not quench them. Finally the contending parties die unreconciled.

For that reason this warning of the apostle still has a significant importance for both men and women in every church of God. An apostolic voice urges them to be ready to rush to the rescue when unexpected quarrels break out between individuals. It urges them to immediately warn and reprimand the contenders, and to extend to them a helpful hand to aid in reconciliation. That voice tells these men and women that they may not abandon their efforts, until that reconciliation has been confirmed at the Table of the Lord.

SUGGESTED QUESTIONS FOR STUDY AND DISCUSSION

1. What women in the New Testament play an important part in the Church of Christ?

2. Was the relation between Euodias and Syntyche always a harmonious one?

3. What do we learn from Paul's teaching with regard to reconciling those at variance?